# FLY TYING
## MADE CLEAR AND SIMPLE

Fly-Tying Illustrations by
Richard Bunse

Skip Morris

Frank Amato Publications
PORTLAND, OREGON

# DEDICATION

I dedicate this book to Paul and Lois Morris who believed in or, when that was not possible, at least accepted their son's notions and dreams, even when those notions and dreams must have seemed odd indeed. They are wonderful people with good hearts.

Richard Bunse Photo

Robyn Restel Photo

# ACKNOWLEDGEMENTS

Along with every fly tier I've ever come in contact with, I'd like to offer my deepest gratitude to the following people: Dave Hughes, Rick Hafele, Richard Bunse, Rod Robinson, Gordon Nash, Brad Burden, Jim Schollmeyer, Randy Stetzer, and Randall Kaufmann for sharing their practical experience with entomology, fly tying, and fly-tying instruction; Byll Davis and Stan Davis (same last name by coincidence, not blood) for their fumble fingers, perseverance, and patience with my endless questions and experiments; Brian Rose for his photographic guidance and skill; Richard Bunse, again, for his excellent illustrations; and Frank Amato for his patience, flexibility, hospitality, wine and pasta.

## RICHARD BUNSE

Richard Bunse, whose illustrations are found within, makes his living through his book illustrations and art. Richard comes from a family of artists; as I write this, he is preparing for an exhibition in California that will feature his work and that of his two brothers. Currently, Richard is illustrating a limited edition of handmade books based on the diaries of angler-writer Roderick Haig-Brown. Many anglers know Richard for his unique foam-body dry-fly patterns.

Richard is an exceptional fly fisher with a special love for the dry fly. He can often be found fishing the streams and lakes near his home in Monmouth, Oregon, a home he shares with his wife Carrol and his two daughters, Robin and Marta.

## BRIAN ROSE

Brian Rose took the materials, tools, and cover photographs for *Fly Tying Made Clear and Simple* and the one of me on the back cover. He is a versatile professional photographer and professional musician specializing in film and video sound-track composition and production. A beginning fly fisher, Brian lives in Portland, Oregon.

10

Copyright ©1992 by Skip Morris

Published in 1992 by Frank Amato Publications,
P.O. Box 82112, Portland, OR 97282.

Softbound: ISBN 1-878175-13-0
Hardbound: ISBN 1-878175-14-9

All photographs taken by the Author except where noted.
Front cover, back cover and photograph on page 1, taken by Brian Rose.
Frontispiece photograph taken by Frank Amato.
Tools and materials for photographs on pages 9, 12, and 13, courtesy of Kaufmann's Streamborn.

Book Design: Tony Amato
Typesetting: Charlie Clifford

Printed in Hong Kong

# CONTENTS

Frank Amato Photo

# FOREWORD

Fly tying is an art. An art that transforms feathers, fur, tinsel, yarn, metal, plastic, leftover sewing materials, rubber bands, thread, floss, and road kill possums into beautiful delicate representations of mayflies, stoneflies, caddisflies, and a thousand other kinds of food fish eat. Like all art it requires imagination—the ability to see a dry fly in a road kill possum is certainly imagination! And it requires certain skills. Proper techniques are the corner stones of any art, and must be mastered before the imagination can be translated into concrete form. To beginners it is the mastery of the basic techniques that can be both frustrating and time consuming if not approached in a clear and simple fashion. For the experienced tyer a review of tying techniques often opens up new ideas and frees the imagination once again.

For thirty years Skip Morris has been tying flies. In *Fly Tying Made Clear and Simple,* Skip takes his extensive experience and lays a foundation of techniques that frees the imagination of both beginner and experienced tyer. I know this first hand, as my own tying has benefitted by just watching Skip tie over the years I have known him. Skip is also an artist. Anyone who has seen Skip's flies understands what I mean. His flies have won many awards, and he is widely recognized as a skillful and innovative tyer.

Without question I believe *Fly Tying Made Clear and Simple* is an innovative book. Innovative not only for the techniques described, but for its approach to teaching fly tying. To find the best way to describe tying methods, Skip went through every technique in this book with two beginning tyers and recorded every question and problem they encountered, then refined his description to make it "clear and simple."

Whether you're starting to tie, or a serious tyer looking for ideas, *Fly Tying Made Clear and Simple* will give you all the necessary techniques for tying quality flies, point out potential problems, and tell you what to do when something goes wrong. Then there is nothing left to do but let your imagination run wild! Happy tying.

**Rick Hafele**
**April 1992**

# INTRODUCTION

Wouldn't it be pleasant if everything went smoothly and easily from the moment we first started tying flies? But fly tying is often challenging, and any fly tier who claims to never have felt hesitation and doubt at the tying vise is a liar, a fool, or a genius. (Smart money is on the first two.)

Though this book is aimed especially at the first-time fly tier, there is much here of value to experienced tiers as we can all use a little help now and then, if not to overcome an obstacle then to improve and grow—how many tiers couldn't wind a neater dry-fly hackle, spin fur bodies more efficiently, or wrap a thread-head more easily and cleanly? After 30 years of performing and honing fly-tying techniques, I am still continually challenged.

I was moved to write *Fly Tying Made Clear and Simple* by my dissatisfaction with other fly-tying books. Some are good, but many offer descriptions too brief for a beginner, too disorganized or unclear for anyone, or simply with no help for those frequent times when things go wrong—tails spin out of position or hair wings refuse to sit upright, neatly gathered. This book includes brief caption-descriptions with each photo, complete descriptions with subheadings, and for those times when things go wrong, advice sections with each step.

The flies in this book were chosen to fulfill two requirements: They must be effective, and they must clearly illustrate at least one fly-tying technique. Once chosen, these flies were arranged into a logical sequence so that you will progress steadily from easy techniques to more advanced ones and so that you will build on and expand each technique as you continue.

Within these pages is all that my years of teaching, professional tying of both fishing and display flies, and learning from other tiers too numerous to list can offer. This last resource must surely be the greatest, and as generous tiers have shared with me, I now share with you. Of the tiers who have helped me, some shared through articles, books, and videos, and some are friends whom I have had the privilege to sit with as they spun a bit of their passion on a hook.

I also owe thanks to my test subjects—the rank beginners who allowed me to hover about them and log their every movement, who patiently struggled through my endless suggestions, experiments, and questions, and who really made the advice and instruction within these pages sound and useful. The other side of this coin is the fact that for every three minutes I spent writing, I spent two tying—in other words, closely observing my own techniques. I have learned, after over a decade as a fly-fishing writer, that the best fly-tying instruction includes plenty of vise-side observation and trial and error.

It is my hope that *Fly Tying Made Clear and Simple* will help pull you out of tight spots for years to come; if it is a book you reach for whenever hesitation and doubt hover about your tying vise, I'll have succeeded.

# Part-I

# FLY TYING ESSENTIALS

## TOOLS

Poor tools are awkward for the experienced fly tier and a beginner's plague. But serviceable tools can be had at modest cost, so anyone should be able to obtain them. In the following section, I have divided tools into two categories: essential and optional. I strongly urge you to skip none of the essential tools. Some of the optional tools are a blessing while others are of questionable value or have value based on the style of the tier using them.

## ESSENTIAL TOOLS

### Vise

A fly-tying vise must have the following qualities if you are to enjoy tying with it: sturdiness, a firm hook hold through a wide range of hooks, ease of tightening and opening, and good tying access to the hook. Such a vise will probably last a lifetime.

Vises either clamp directly onto a tabletop or have their own portable base. The sturdiest setup is the clamp mount, but a good base-mount vise is sturdy enough and awfully convenient—I used clamp-mount vises for years but now use a base-mount. Both are good if well made and well designed. Either sound advice or a hands-on test will help you determine a vise's sturdiness.

A really firm hook hold is a must. Once a hook is locked in the jaws, tying pressure should deform it before it slips; the exception might be really big hooks of unusually heavy wire. Lock a hook firmly in a vise and push down hard on the hook's eye (the tiny ring of wire at one end of the hook)—if the hook bends but stays put, fine; but if it slips, pass on that vise. Also, test to see if the vise will hold both tiny and big hooks; for the beginner, this kind of versatility is important. Some vises have more than one set of jaws in order to fully accommodate the broad range of hook sizes. Special big-fly or tiny-fly vises are a boon to the experienced tier but are too restrictive for the beginner.

The jaws of a fly-tying vise are tightened in a variety of ways: turning a knob, pushing a lever, or releasing a lever to name a few. The main point is that however the jaws tighten, they should do so smoothly and easily and open the same way. I have only owned one vise with jaws that were difficult to open and close, but I wound up doing so with a pair of pliers before I finally gave up and bought another vise.

Most vises offer plenty of tying access for all but the tiniest hooks. But bulky, thick jaws, or a tightening lever too close to the hook can make tying awkward.

Finally, you must decide whether to buy a stationary or a rotary vise. A stationary vise is, essentially, stationary (makes sense to me); a rotary vise will swivel to allow you to tie or observe the fly from various angles. For years I tied on a stationary vise, even tied flies that won contests with it, but now I wouldn't give up my rotary. Rotary vises usually cost considerably more than stationary ones. A good compromise would be to start on a serviceable-but-inexpensive stationary vise, and then delegate it as your on-stream and travelling vise when you later buy a rotary.

### Hackle Pliers

These clamp onto the end of a feather called a "hackle" which is then wound around a hook. Most hackle pliers have a loop which the tier inserts a finger through. Some pliers have no loop, and some tiers prefer this. I suggest you start with the loop kind.

The standard jaws for hackle pliers are rounded and metal. Some pliers have rubber pads and some even have a tiny wire hook to catch the hackle's tip. The standard rounded, metal-jawed pliers have always served me so well that I've never really tried the other types.

I have no love for miniature hackle pliers supposedly useful for tying tiny flies; I find them awkward, and I can't get my finger into their loops.

### Hackle Gauge

This item almost slipped into the "optional" category; after all, fly tiers, myself included, used the old wrap-the-hackle-around-the-hook hackle-sizing method for a long time before gauges came along. The only problem is that it didn't work very well. I can't imagine not using a gauge now.

There are fine gauges on the market, but you can make your own with a little ingenuity. You just need to work out something that has a post to curve a hackle around and some marks to indicate fiber length. More about hackle sizing can be found under "The Woolly Bugger" and "The Adams."

### Bobbins

There are thread bobbins and floss bobbins. Of the two, only the thread bobbin is an essential tool. It will be discussed here, and the floss bobbin will be discussed in the next section.

One good thread bobbin is indispensable. You can switch spools easily, and therefore thread colors and sizes; so one thread bobbin is plenty to begin with. Some bobbins have frames that angle the spool so the thread goes straight into the tube—no corners to slip around. This is a good idea because there is nothing to stress and weaken the thread. But bobbins that put the spool dead center are

# TOOLS

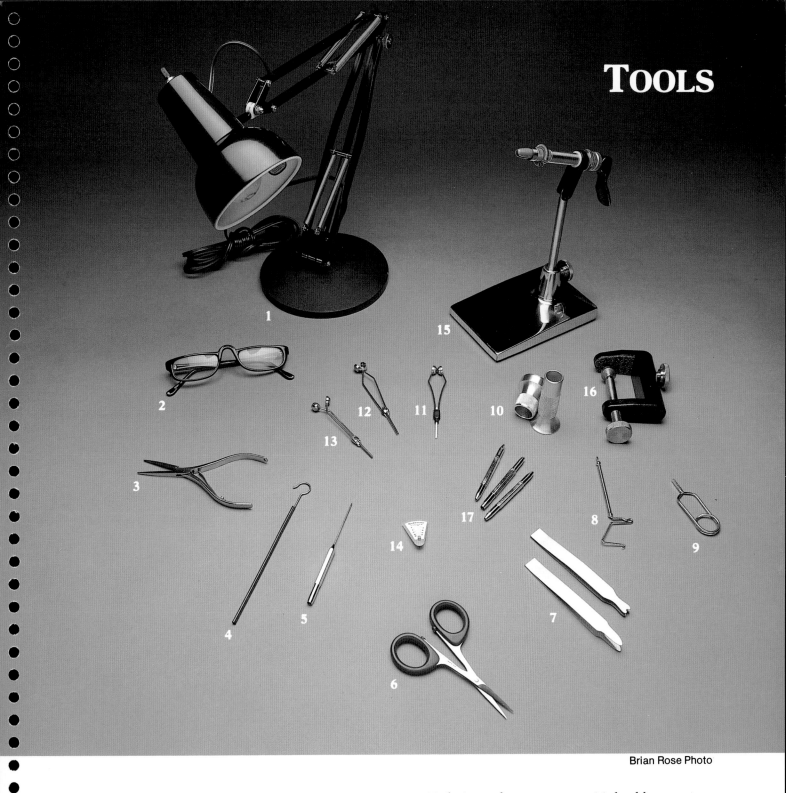

1. lamp
2. magnifying glasses
3. flat nosed pliers
4. dubbing twister
5. bodkin

6. scissors
7. wing burners
8. whip finisher
9. hackle pliers

10. hair stacker
11. ceramic bobbin
12. floss bobbin
13. all-metal bobbin

14. hackle gauge
15. HMH base vise
16. C-clamp for vise
17. half-hitch tools

symmetrical, which means you can spin them easily to twist the thread; twisting thread is rarely necessary, but occasionally thread will flatten and splay more than you'll want, and then twisting will gather it.

Ceramic-tube bobbins are supposedly less likely to fray or cut thread than conventional metal-tube bobbins. I haven't been using ceramic bobbins for long, so I can't say I've noticed a difference yet—but some of my friends who have used them since they first came out swear by them. If ceramic bobbins truly last longer than metal-tube bobbins, that alone could be good reason to consider them.

## Light

A strong well-focused overhead light is important—without it you will constantly strain your eyes. Good ambient light also helps. My light is a modestly priced, adjustable jointed-arm type. I bring it down within only a few inches of my work. It holds a standard 100 watt light bulb.

## Hair Stacker

Another near miss for the "optional" list. A hair stacker evens and squares the tips of various hairs; it does this when you tap it—the hairs all slip down and stop with their tips against a flat, removable cap. You can hand stack hair, and sometimes this is best, but when you really want well-stacked hair, which is often, there is no better solution than a hair stacker. Get a stacker with a large opening—it is the separation of the hairs that allows them to stack, and small hair bunches can be regathered by tilting the stacker a bit during the last tap or two.

## Scissors

Buy a good pair of fly-tying scissors; any not specifically designed for fly tying won't make it. The best fly-tying scissors have finely serrated blades which keep materials from slipping. Be certain the scissors you buy have adequate room in their loops for your fingers.

## OPTIONAL TOOLS

## Pliers

These are for pinching down hook barbs to protect fish you want to release unharmed. Nowadays, most fly fishers release most or all of their fish. Some fly-fishing-only waters *require* that barbs are pinched down. I put pliers under the "optional" heading because some fly tiers buy barbless hooks and others find alternate ways to make their hooks barbless. Still, the majority of fly fishers pinch down their barbs with pliers. Pliers for pinching barbs should have fine, flat-surfaced jaws that will handle even the tiniest hooks.

## Toothpicks

For my own tying, toothpicks are essential. I use them mostly for adding head cement, a procedure used on every fly. Toothpicks are also handy for teasing fur, freeing trapped hackle fibers, clearing hook eyes, and a number of other uses that will make more sense as you progress through this book. Buy the round toothpicks with sharp points.

## Bodkin

Many fly tiers swear by a bodkin. It is essentially a needle on a handle. You will be amazed at how often it comes in handy. Usually, however, I can do a bodkin's work with a toothpick. For those times when I have to have a bodkin, I use a hatpin.

## Dubbing Twister

Though you won't need one for the flies in this book, dubbing twisters are sometimes handy. They allow you to build a really thick fur body. There are good commercially made dubbing twisters, or you can make one by straightening out one end of a paper clip.

## Blender

For blending various colors and types of fur, blenders are wonderful. You can blend furs with water in a household electric blender, or you can blend quite satisfactorily, though slowly, by hand. But the neatest, easiest way of all is to blend in a dry blender, which is available through many fly shops.

## Floss Bobbin

Although it is quite similar to a thread bobbin, a floss bobbin has a wider tube with flared ends and is designed to handle floss or other spooled materials. A floss bobbin is not a necessity, but a floss bobbin can make tying quicker and waste less materials than hand wrapping.

## Old Scissors
### (or fingernail clippers)

For cutting hard materials—lead, copper wire, thick quills—a pair of old scissors really helps. You must never cut hard materials with the tips of your regular scissors although you can use the inner parts of their blades—but with old scissors who cares? If you haven't yet tied long enough to have old scissors, get some cheap ones or a pair of fingernail clippers.

## Material Holder

These are very helpful; they attach to your vise just behind its jaws and hold long materials out of your way. Some vises come already mounted with a material holder. My favorite material holder is the spring type in which a spring is wrapped around the vise and the materials slip down into the coils.

## Magnifier

This means either magnifying glasses or a large lens on an adjustable arm. Many of the arm-mounted lenses have their own lighting built in. I use magnification all the time when tying display-quality flies, but with fishing flies I only use magnification occasionally. Tiny trout flies are another matter—these are standard fare for today's trout fishing, and magnification really helps in their tying. The tier whose eyes have seen quite a few years may find magnifiers a boon for all tying.

## Whip Finisher

Whip finishers come in various styles, and all come with instructions. These tools aid in executing the "whip finish," the final knot that secures a fly's head. I prefer to execute my whip finishes by hand, but some good tiers swear by these tools. I suggest you learn the manual whip finish before purchasing a whip finisher.

## Half-Hitch Tool

Almost everything I just said for the whip finisher goes for the half-hitch tool; the only exceptions are that there seems to be only one basic style and that the half-hitch tool is even less essential than the whip finisher.

## Wing Burners

These allow you to burn feathers to wing shapes. Most flies don't call for burnt wings and most anglers don't bother with them. But burnt wings look great, surely to anglers and possibly to trout, and wing burners are fun to play with.

## Bobbin Threader

This consists of a wire loop that slips down a bobbin's tube to draw out the thread. The same thing can be accomplished with a creased loop of nylon leader or by sucking the thread down the tube. Bobbin threaders work very well, but I have heard rumors that their wire loops can scratch the inside of the bobbin's tube which in turn frays and weakens thread.

## Hair Packers (compressors)

Hair packers simply compress spun hair, and a dense packing with spun hair is desirable. I prefer to use my thumb and finger for the same duty because I can pack hair best this way. But if you aren't too worried about how tightly your spun hair is packed and you find yourself with sore fingers from hand packing, use a hair packer.

---

# MATERIALS

My usage of the word "materials" includes almost anything that ends up in a fly: feathers, fur, thread, wire, synthetics and even the cement that holds everything secure. Most fly tiers use the word in the same way. Not all the materials used in fly tying are covered here—to do so would require a volume of its own, since creative fly tiers have always added generously to the sum—but all of the materials used in this book, and all those most commonly used, are explored here.

## Threads

Fly-tying thread comes in several sizes—and many colors—for a variety of purposes and tastes. Let's cover sizes first. The most commonly used are the threads for tying average-size trout flies—threads of sizes 8/0 and 6/0. At this writing 8/0 is a newcomer, but I like it; it seems as strong as 6/0, but is finer and splays less. 6/0 is the traditional choice. 8/0 is fine enough for even tiny flies, but there are also special extra-fine threads for this. Extra-fine threads require a light, even touch though, as they break easily—I would suggest you use 8/0 for your tiny flies to begin with. 3/0 is a heavy thread for big flies; it's tough. When very tight thread tension is required, 3/0 makes sense. I also use size A nylon rod-winding thread for spinning deer hair, a technique more common to bass-bug tying than trout-fly tying.

Thread colors are many; each manufacturer has its own variations. I don't consider thread color a big issue. The yellow thread-head of a Partridge and Yellow Soft Hackle echoes the yellow body and pleases the angler's eye, but the trout won't care if the head is tan or even brown. A good place to start is with two thread colors: light (tan is good) and dark (a brown or even black).

Fly-tying thread comes either prewaxed or unwaxed. Prewaxed thread is generally lightly waxed and is my first choice. Additional wax may be added to prewaxed thread for certain procedures.

## Wax

Wax is used for waxing thread; wax is optional but handy. Most tiers now use soft waxes, but hard waxes are fine.

## Lead

Lead wire is often added to wet flies to get them down. The finest lead is for little flies (every catalog seems to rate the thickness of lead wire in a different way, so I'll keep this general). Lead wire of medium thickness is what I use the majority of the time—I can usually squeeze it into little flies, and for big flies I just add all I need. The thickest lead wire is sometimes useful for really big flies. For tiny flies, only fine lead wire will do.

# MATERIALS

Brian Rose Photo

1. dyed bucktail
2. natural bucktail
3. Tuffilm
4. epoxy head cement
5. marking pens
6. dyed calf tail
7. natural calf tail
8. red fox squirrel tail
9. gray squirrel tail
10. floss
11. head cement

12. Dave's flexament
13. tying threads
14. lead wire
15. tinsels and wires
16. Fly Bright
17. Edge Bright
18. antron yarn
19. poly yarn
20. large chenille
21. medium chenille

22. Ocean Hair
23. Flashabou
24. Krystal Flash
25. rubber hackle
26. moose mane
27. moose body
28. antron dubbing
29. evasote
30. poly dubbing
31. Larva Lace

32. Swannundaze
33. V-rib
34. Microfibetts
35. Barbetts
36. dubbing wax
37. natural light elk
38. coastal deer
39. caribou
40. dyed deer
41. natural deer

Brian Rose Photo

| | | | |
|---|---|---|---|
| 1. ostrich | 9. teal flank | 17. muskrat | 25. dyed green grizzly hackle |
| 2. peacock | 10. wood duck | 18. red fox | 26. rooster |
| 3. marabou plumes | 11. mallard flank | 19. woodchuck | 27. ginger dry fly hackle cape |
| 4. turkey flat | 12. mallard quills | 20. mole | 28. brown dry fly hackle cape |
| 5. guinea | 13. turkey quills | 21. hare's mask | 29. grizzly dry fly hackle cape |
| 6. jungle cock eyes | 14. angora goat | 22. hen saddle | 30. dark blue dun dry fly hackle cape |
| 7. partridge | 15. beaver | 23. dyed hen neck | 31. light blue dun dry fly hackle cape |
| 8. English grouse | 16. badger | 24. strung saddle hackles | 32. white dry fly hackle cape |

# Feathers

**Hackles:** These come from different parts of roosters and chickens; the type of hackle chosen depends upon how the fly tier plans to use it. The most expensive hackles are the domestic dry-fly neck hackles (which do in fact come right from the neck and back of the rooster); these roosters are specially bred to grow long neck hackles with stiff, bright fibers of constant length and with slender stems.

A dry-fly hackle is wound around a hook to create a fiber collar; a dry-fly hackle's fibers may also be used for tails. Some roosters are bred to produce hackles especially for making the wings of a fly called a "streamer." Saddle hackle comes from the rump, and the finest rooster saddles make fine dry-fly hackles, though it's hard to get a full range of hackle sizes in saddles. Rooster saddle hackles are also used for making wings for various sunk flies. Hen hackles, both neck and saddle, have lots of uses—dry-fly wings, nymph legs, and sunk-fly collars to name a few.

Hackles come in many different colors and with a variety of markings. For dry-fly work, I suggest you start with one light-colored neck (most dry-fly hackles come attached to the skin, all of which is collectively called a "neck") and one dark-colored one; a ginger neck and a brown neck would be good. If the fly calls for a blue dun hackle collar, this is dark, so the brown would be close enough; for white or light blue dun, substitute the ginger. The third dry-fly hackle neck you buy should be a grizzly—in fact if you buy only one neck to start, the grizzly would be best.

There is a broad number of hackle colors and markings. Here are the standard variations:

**Grizzly**—alternating white and black bars or stripes across the feather.

**Ginger**—light ginger is pale, even almost cream, and dark ginger is a golden tan.

**Brown**—brown, sometimes reddish.

**Blue dun**—a bluish gray; from pale to dark.

**Badger**—cream to tan with a black, tapered stripe running up the center along the stem.

**Furnace**—same as badger but darker, some kind of brown with a black stripe.

**White**—white.

**Cream**—cream.

**Primaries:** These are large wing feathers. Duck primaries and brown mottled turkey primaries are frequently called for in dry-fly wings and the wing cases of nymphs. (Primaries are often called "quills.")

**Body Feathers:** Simply feathers that are not primaries and are from some part of a bird other than the neck. In my experience, these are the most commonly called-for body feathers: partridge, grouse, mallard, wood duck, guinea, turkey, and teal.

**Herls:** The most common ones come from peacock, followed by ostrich. Herls come from the handsome fan-like tail feathers, and are usually sold on the feather. Usually, herls are wrapped to create a fuzzy body, but they can also be used in sinking-fly wings.

**Marabou:** This is a downy soft plume that is most frequently used in the wings or long, full tails of sunk flies. It comes dyed in many colors.

**Pheasant Tail:** The fibers from a pheasant tail are tough, handsome, and natural looking. They are also very useful to the tier.

**Jungle Cock:** These exotic feathers create the appearance of eyes on some flies. The high cost of jungle cock has driven many tiers to substitutes, or to discard jungle-cock features altogether.

# Hair And Fur

**Hollow Hair:** "Hollow" is usually the word used to describe hairs that have tiny air pockets within. The pockets give these hairs two desirable qualities: buoyancy and a spongy consistency. Buoyancy is clearly of value for a floating fly. The consistency of hollow hair allows the tier to flare it and then shape it—a technique used more often in bass bugs than in trout flies. Hollow hair is excellent for dry-fly wings and tails.

Deer-body hair is the all-around hollow hair. Elk is a bit coarser, which is sometimes desirable. Caribou is the finest and spongiest, but it is also the most fragile of the hollow hairs commonly used in fly tying.

The density of deer hair often determines its use—the hair that flares so well for bass-bug bodies may flare too much for dry-fly wings. Sometimes the source of deer hair is identified in its labeling to inform the tier of its consistency ("coastal deer," for example, is too hard for good flaring but excellent for wings). Usually, however, the tier chooses by appearance and feel or with the help of a fly-shop or fly-fishing mail-order-house salesperson.

**Bucktail:** This provides long, hard hairs for the wings of dry flies and especially for the wings of "bucktail" flies—hair-winged flies that are swum to suggest bait fish and other aquatic creatures.

**Calf Tail:** The kinky haired version of bucktail—very useful.

**Squirrel Tail:** Naturally either gray or reddish brown. Softer and finer than bucktail, but similar overall.

**Moose Body:** Great dry-fly tail material and good for dry-fly wings. Color is dark gray.

**Moose Mane:** Like moose body hair but coarser and more brittle.

**Furs:** There are a variety of furs used in fly tying including the following: rabbit, goat, badger, hare's mask, beaver, otter, muskrat, opossum, and red fox—and these are just the standards. Furs are usually spun onto tying thread and then wrapped around hooks to form fly bodies. The heavy guard hairs of some furs—badger and hare's mask for example—can be separated from the soft under-fur for fly wings, fly tails or both. Some flies now use furs on the hide. I am pleased to say that new uses for fur are coming along all the time—innovation is half the fun. Fur fly bodies can also be formed with synthetic fur which will be discussed later.

## Yarns, Chenilles, And Flosses

**Yarns:** These are traditional and still useful. Wool yarn is the old standby, but all kinds of yarns are now available; some offer fuzziness and others, sparkle. Many of the newer yarns are composed entirely of synthetic fibers or are a blend of natural and synthetic. Yarns, depending on type, are used for either sinking flies, dry flies, or both.

**Chenille:** Fibers woven into a thread core to create a thick, fuzzy rope. Chenille comes in various sizes and countless colors. To this day, chenille remains a popular body material for sinking flies.

**Floss:** Avialable in lots of colors. Floss creates a fine, smooth body. Because it doesn't offer much buoyancy, floss is usually used on sinking flies nowadays. You can get four-strand, two-strand or single-strand floss; most of the time, I prefer the single-strand because I find it easiest to control. All floss used to be made of silk; now it is almost always made of rayon.

## Synthetic Materials

Some of the materials we have already discussed are synthetics—floss, mylar tinsel. Synthetics seem to come and go rapidly these days, but many are really useful.

Poly dubbing is a synthetic dubbing fur that is now well established. Poly yarn is tough and buoyant. Swannundaze, Larva Lace, and "V" Rib (among others) are hard, gelatinous-looking ribbing materials that are used frequently for flies that imitate underwater insects.

Micro Fibetts and Barbetts are synthetic realistic tail fibers. Foam rubber is marketed under several brand names and is proving excellent for dry-fly bodies. Rubber hackle (also called "rubber legs") is similar to strips of rubber-band material and is used especially in bass flies. Synthetic materials used for long wings of flies that swim, and synthetic body materials for these same flies abound; here is a sample list: Krystal Flash, Frostbite, Flashabou, Edge Bright, Fly Bright, Ocean Hair.

## Tinsels

All tinsel used to be composed of metal; now it is often composed of a synthetic called "mylar." Tinsels usually come in silver or gold, but some new colors, including an interesting pearl, are finding their place in fly tying.

Tinsels may be flat and of various widths, oval and of various diameters, woven into a tube, "embossed" (having a pattern raised on the surface), or braided—each has its place.

Wires are close cousins of tinsels. There are silver, gold, and copper wires (and new ones showing up) in various diameters. Wires are often called for in nymph fly patterns and are sometimes even used in dry flies. Most tinsel and wire is spiraled down a fly's body as "ribbing."

## Marking Pens

Waterproof marking pens are still in the beginning stages of fly-tying application; expect to see their usage increase. These pens come in a great diversity of types and colors. Fly shops often carry them as do artist's supply stores.

## Cements

Those most often used by fly tiers are "head cements"—glues or cements added to the finishing knot of tying thread that holds the fly together. Head cements come in various forms, but most are a liquid that air cures. My favorite head cement is a two-part rod-builder's epoxy glue (see "Cementing the Head" under "Rick's Caddis"). Other glues and cements are used to reinforce fragile materials, add gloss, or simply enhance durability; Dave's Flexament and Tuffilm are two of the most common. (Tuffilm is a toughening spray that can be obtained through artist's supply stores.)

---

# HOOKS SIMPLIFIED

---

To understand hooks, it is best to start with a bit of anatomy. The "eye" is the loop of wire at one end of a hook; the "shank" is a hook's long, straight middle section; the "bend" is the widely curved wire at the opposite end from the eye; the "point" is the sharp, penetrating point at the end of the bend; the "gap," also called a "gape," is the distance between the hook's point and shank; and the "barb" is the tiny upturned shard, just behind the point, that is meant to keep a hook from slipping out of a fish (a suspect theory we will soon discuss further).

There are only three basic considerations for selecting a hook: size, length, and wire. Other considerations

are minor, and usually subjective, though we will explore them as well. But first let's take a look at the basic three.

Hooks are sized by numbers. The numbers are almost always even (though a very few hooks are sized with odd numbers, for reasons I fail to understand). The tiniest hooks have the largest numbers—a size 14 hook is about average for trout flies, a size 20 is tiny, and a size 26 is so small that most anglers will never tie or fish with one. Big trout hooks start at size 8, but past size 1, the sizing starts at 1/0 and from that point on, hooks get *larger* as their numbers get larger—I'm sorry, but they do. From 1/0 on up, the "/0" follows each number. You won't have to worry about anything with an "/0" behind it in this book.

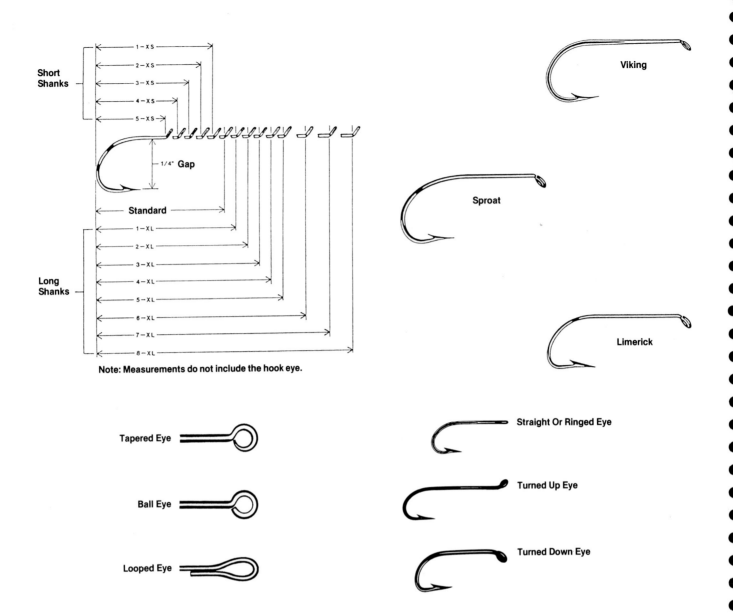

Short Shanks
- 1 – X S
- 2 – X S
- 3 – X S
- 4 – X S
- 5 – X S

1/4" Gap

Standard

Long Shanks
- 1 – X L
- 2 – X L
- 3 – X L
- 4 – X L
- 5 – X L
- 6 – X L
- 7 – X L
- 8 – X L

Note: Measurements do not include the hook eye.

Viking

Sproat

Limerick

Tapered Eye

Ball Eye

Looped Eye

Straight Or Ringed Eye

Turned Up Eye

Turned Down Eye

## MUSTAD HOOK COMPARISON CHART

| Fly | Hook Shown | Closest Mustad Hook |
|---|---|---|
| Rick's Caddis | Dai-Riki 730 | 9671 |
| Woolly Bugger | Tiemco 9395 | 79580 |
| Gold Ribbed Hare's Ear | Daiichi 1550 | 3906 |
| Morristone | Partridge Grey Shadow GRS 4A | 9672 |
| Pheasant Tail | Eagle Claw D57 | 3906 |
| Skip Nymph Dark | Partridge Captain Hamilton H1A | 3906B |
| Micky Finn | Dai-Riki 700 | 79580 |
| Black Ghost | Gamakutsu F16 | 79580 |
| Partridge and Yellow Soft Hackle | Daiichi 1180 | 94840 |
| Adams | Mustad 94840 | same |
| Gray Wulff | Gamakutsu F13 | 94840 |
| Elk Hair Caddis | Tiemco 100 | 94840 |
| Comparadun | Eagle Claw D59 | 94840 |
| Light Cahill Parachute | Partridge Grey Shadow Captain Hamilton GRS3A | 94840 |
| Griffith's Gnat | Mustad 94859 | same |

Hook length is signified with a number, followed by an "X," followed by a "long" or "short." The explanation is that there is a standard length for each hook size and that the numbers, "X"s, and "long"s and "short"s tell you how far, and in which direction, a hook deviates from that standard. If your hook is "standard length" or "regular length," that's obvious. However, if your hook is 1X long, that means that your hook is one size longer than regular length—but what does *that* mean? In theory, it means that this hook is the same length as a hook one size larger; but in fact, it means whatever that particular manufacturer says it means. What is significant is that a hook 1X long is slightly longer than normal, a hook 2X long is slightly longer yet, and a hook 8X long is really long. All this works in reverse for the "short" designations—"1X short" is slightly short and "2X short" is slightly shorter and so on. Hook length does not affect the hook's bend or gape; they remain constant, and the hook's eye isn't a consideration in determining length.

Hook wire is usually chosen to help a fly sink or float—thick wire is heavy and makes a fly sink; thin wire is lighter and helps a fly float. Occasionally thick wire is chosen simply for strength; this usually means big, powerful fish—bass, tarpon, and the like. Thin wire is called "fine" and thick wire is called "heavy." The fineness or heaviness of wire is determined, once again, with "X"s, and once again, all this begins with the assumption that there is a model, an acknowledged norm—in this case, a standard hook wire for each hook size. And "standard" is the word for it—a hook with wire between fine and heavy has "standard wire." "1X heavy" means a hook with wire meant for a hook one size larger, "2X heavy" for a hook two sizes larger, "1X light" for a hook one size smaller and so on. This business too, I suspect, varies from one manufacturer to the next.

So how do you decide exactly the size, length, and wire thickness of your hook? Easy: follow the pattern. A "pattern" is simply a list-description of materials for a given fly; more on this later.

Time for a review. If your fly's pattern calls for a hook that is size 12, 2X long, 1X heavy, what does this mean? Stop and try to answer this before you read on. Here is what it means: The hook you want is of about average size for trout, it is two increments longer than the standard, and it is formed of wire that would normally be used on a hook one size larger. How did you do?

There are some secondary hook considerations, but although there are accepted guidelines to cover them, most experienced fly tiers decide for themselves. The hooks designated for the flies in this book generally conform to these guidelines. The first of these secondary considerations is the angle of the eye. If the eye tips up, it is an "up eye" or "turned up-eye"; if the eye is straight, in line with the shank, it is a "ring eye"; if the eye tips down, it is a "down eye" or "turned down eye." Everyone used to use turned-down-eye hooks for almost everything except Atlantic salmon and steelhead, but a lot of anglers now use the other eye styles for all kinds of fishing—personal preference. There are also variations in eye construction, but I've found them usually to be of only minor significance, and if a special eye style is important for a certain type of fishing—the tapered loop-eye of Atlantic-salmon and steelhead hooks is a good example—you'll hear about it plenty.

Another secondary consideration is the shape of the bend. There are "Limerick," "Perfect," "Sneck," and "Sproat" bends and these sometimes go by different names. There are probably other bends of which I am unaware. The pattern may advise, but anglers usually make this a personal decision. As Dave Hughes wrote in his *American Fly Tying Manual*, "Hook bends are mostly a matter of eye appeal, though there are endless debates about the hooking qualities of each kind....The Viking, Sproat, and Limerick are the three most popular styles; they've all been around for years, and they all hook and hold fish well."

Watch for abbreviations. "1X short" may become "1XS," "2X light" may be "2XL," "turned up eye" may be "TUE" and so on. But it's all pretty logical.

There is also the matter of manufacturers who disregard the rules. You look through their catalogs for a 6X long hook and the only thing close says "streamer-bucktail hook"; that's alright though, because you are tying a streamer. If you needed the 6X long for a big nymph there is still no problem, because even a little experience will tell you that a streamer hook is just a long nymph hook, more or less. The bottom line is this: First, hook choices are mostly subjective; second, hook manufacturers are not in all that much agreement anyway, so precise designations have varying meanings; and third, a bit of experience, or advice, and especially a glance at the hook or its picture will make the decision an easy one.

Finally, there are the hooks too odd to really fit into the system. Such hooks include "stinger," "caddis pupa," and "Swedish dry fly" types among others. Another way in which manufacturers create odd hooks is simply by giving them odd specifications. Perhaps there is something I am missing here, but isn't a hook designated as "wide gap" the same as a hook with a short shank? Odd hooks have their place, but most anglers still use conventional hooks, that *do* fit the system, the vast majority of the time.

The chart on page 16 may well be obsolete by the time this book is in print. Why might this chart become obsolete? To understand this, I'd best take you back a few years. Not long ago, almost everyone used Mustad hooks for almost everything; some used Partridge hooks for some things. Suddenly, in the 1980s, there were hook companies galore. Each new company had its own model number or name for each hook style. Anglers were confused; they were used to the Mustad model numbers which meant nothing with the new hooks. The fact is, we will all have to get used to the hook-classification system eventually. But for those who still think Mustad, the chart will show you how the hooks in this book compare with those of that venerable company.

# Part-II
# NYMPHS AND THE WOOLLY BUGGER

## COMPONENTS OF AN ARTIFICIAL NYMPH

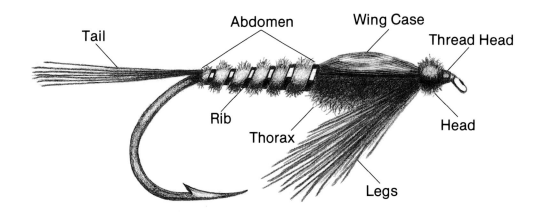

Tail · Abdomen · Wing Case · Thread Head · Rib · Thorax · Head · Legs

## COMPONENTS OF A WOOLLY BUGGER

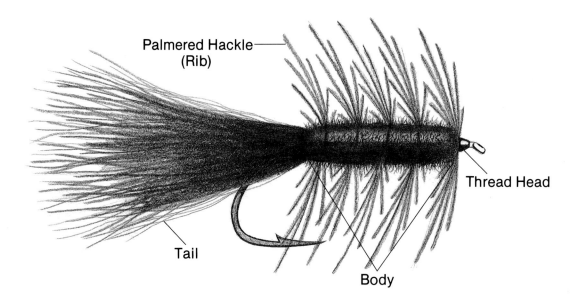

Palmered Hackle (Rib) · Thread Head · Tail · Body

Illustrations by Tony Amato

Originally, the term "nymph" referred to the immature form of some aquatic insects. Other aquatic insects have two forms in place of the nymph: "larva" and "pupa." Some aquatic insects have none of these. To an "entomologist," one who studies insects, a nymph is still a nymph, but fly fishers have broadened the use of the term.

To a fly fisher, a nymph is an insect that lives underwater or an *imitation* of an insect that lives underwater. So even if a fly imitates a larva or a pupa—or practically anything that even resembles an underwater insect—fly fishers will probably call that fly a nymph.

Nymph-imitating flies are the best place to begin the study of fly tying because many are simple and easy to tie. The second fly you'll tie, the Woolly Bugger, is closer to a streamer and should technically be in the next section of this book. But it is here because this is the best place for it in the tying sequence, and that's what really matters.

# RICK'S CADDIS

The Rick's Caddis imitates the immature form of an important trout-food insect: the caddisfly. My friend Rick Hafele, professional entomologist and writer of fly-fishing books and articles, developed the original bright-green version of this fly to match the larva of the *Rhyocophilia* caddis, commonly called the green rockworm. But the Rick's Caddis can be tied in a variety of colors, sizes, and even materials, to suggest many other caddisfly larva. This fly is usually fished along stream beds "dead drift"—adrift in the current with no imparted motion from the angler.

The Rick's Caddis will familiarize you with a fly-tying technique that was in common use long before I was born and that continues to grow more widespread in its use: dubbing. The word "dubbing" has two distinct meanings to the fly tier: There is dubbing, the material, which is natural or synthetic fur spun onto tying thread; and there is dubbing, the action, which is the process of creating a fly body of fur. Therefore, you will soon be using dubbing for dubbing your Rick's Caddis. Here you will also learn to handle lead.

If you are a beginning fly tier, or an experienced one who might benefit by re-examining the basics, be certain you read this section because in it we will establish fundamental procedures used throughout this book.

The listing of fly name, hook size and type, and materials is called a "pattern." In most cases a pattern is all an experienced tier needs in order to tie a particular fly. Once you understand the basic techniques and terminology of fly tying, a pattern is all *you* will need, and by the time you finish this book, following a pattern will be second nature.

## Essential Guidelines

Before we begin tying, these simple guidelines will prove a big help; as you tie, keep them in mind.

1. Always wrap thread (or anything else that wraps unless instructed otherwise) away from you over the hook, and toward you beneath the hook.

2. While wrapping thread or materials, remember to dodge the hook's sharp point.

3. Try to maintain constant thread tension throughout the tying of a fly (except for those special procedures that require momentary slack), because even a split second of

slack at a critical point can leave a fly hopelessly loose and fragile.

4. Most hooks (especially light-wire dry-fly hooks and long-shank streamer hooks) are flexible and will need added support occasionally—just grasp the hook and hold it firmly as needed.

5. If your thread breaks, simply clamp your hackle pliers onto the loose end, let them hang, start the thread again, wrap back over the old thread end, trim both the old and new thread ends, and continue tying as usual.

6. Unless you need extra free thread for a specific procedure, try to keep the bobbin near the fly—a long stretch of thread between hook and bobbin is terribly inefficient and seems always in the way.

7. Your vise can function as a steady rest, especially when using your scissors; lean your hand, or just one or two fingers, against your vice, or steady one hand against the vise and the other hand against that hand.

8. A properly adjusted bobbin is generally pretty tight—sometimes it is best to adjust the amount of thread between bobbin and hook by holding the bobbin in one hand and rotating the thread spool with the other.

9. Wrapping something "forward" means toward the hook's eye, and "back" or "rearward" means toward the hook's bend. When I refer to the "front" of a hook or fly, I am referring to the end with the hook's eye; when I refer to the "rear," I am referring to the end where the bend begins, from which the tail often projects. If you show horses in competition, this should be easy to remember, as they generally have their eyes in the front and their tails at the rear, and any horse without this arrangement will show poorly.

10. If I tell you to tie in something at, or wrap back to, the "bend," I am referring to the place at the rear of the hook where the hook's straight shank meets the first curve of its bend.

11. Unless otherwise noted, instructions will be for the right-handed. This leaves left-handers to make the necessary adjustments—a skill at which left-handers are most adept, a necessity in a right-handed world.

**RICK'S CADDIS** *(Rhyocophila)*

**Hook:** Any 1X or 2X long, heavy-wire hook, sizes 16 to 10. (Also, there are now a variety of special hooks made especially for caddis larva; the original of these is called the English bait hook.)
**Thread:** Brown, 8/0 or 6/0.
**Weight:** For hook sizes 14 and larger, No. 2 lead; for hooks size 16 and smaller, No. 1 lead.
**Abdomen:** Bright green natural or synthetic fur. (Many other colors may be used to imitate other caddis species and Rick sometimes uses other body materials.)
**Thorax:** Brown natural or synthetic fur.

1. Threading the bobbin with a bobbin threader (note the wire loop of the threader and the thread end in it).

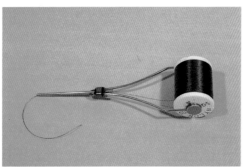

2. A properly threaded bobbin (the thread shown is actually a heavy rod-winding thread that was used because I knew it would show up well in the photograph).

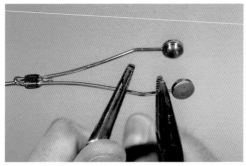

3. Adjusting the bobbin's frame.

## Threading The Bobbin

First, you need to thread your bobbin. To begin, free the end of the thread from its notch in the spool. Mount the spool in the bobbin, draw off 6 to 8 inches of thread and put its end into the back of the bobbin's tube, the end of the tube nearest the spool. Suck a quick blast of air from the other end of the tube and the thread end will reappear. This is the method I generally use, but many prefer to push a folded piece of nylon fishing line or the end of a commercially made bobbin threader down the tube, pass the thread end through the looped end of the line or threader, and pull everything back through.

## Threading The Bobbin — Problems, Solutions, And Suggestions

1. Finding the end of the thread can be tricky; look for a strand that cuts across the others at an angle.
2. Look for a notch in one of the spool's rims; the thread end should be there.
3. Work the thread end loose with your scissor's tips. Sometimes you will have to cut the thread end if it won't pry free.
4. If the thread end won't suck through the bobbin tube, it's probably because the tube is plugged with wax (clear it with stiff, heavy fishing line or something similar), or because the thread end is frayed (snip it off clean).

## Adjusting The Bobbin

The thread should draw from your bobbin under modest tension; this gives you control over thread tension by squeezing the spool hard, lightly, or not at all. You can adjust the bobbin now, or you can wait until you've tied for awhile. If you wait, see if the bobbin is so tight that it breaks your thread or if it is so loose that thread is always slipping out of it against your wishes—in either case, the bobbin will need adjusting. Some bobbins adjust with tightening knobs, but most adjust by carefully bending their frame. Pliers help. But as you bend the frame, absolutely avoid putting pressure on the connection between the frame and the tube—if that connection breaks, your bobbin is probably ruined.

## Smashing The Barb

Select a size 14, 2X long heavy-wire hook or, as an alternate, a size-12 1X long hook. Bear in mind that a fly is tied on a hook's shank, so the longer the shank, the larger the fly, even though the number size of the hook stays constant. The size-14, 2X long hook I have suggested will therefore support the same size fly as a 1X long size-12 hook and a standard-length size-10 hook—the point is, if you want to use a 1X long hook, and produce a fly of the same size as the one shown, make your 1X-long hook a size 12. Of course, you could use a hook of the humped English bait style, but to begin with I suggest a conventional hook. (The hook shown is a Dai-Riki, model 730.) As the pattern indicates, there is a range of possible hook sizes for the Ricks Caddis, but a size-14 hook is a good place to start.

Most fly fishers smash the barbs on their hooks to insure the safe release of fish; I strongly recommend smashing your barbs.

To smash the barb simply press it firmly down between the jaws of a pair of flat-nosed pliers; modest force will do it. Avoid pliers with serrated or rounded jaws if possible, as these may damage the hook or just not do the job. Some fly shops now carry inexpensive pliers for smashing hook barbs.

## Mounting The Hook In Your Vise

Lock the hook into your vise as shown—not so deeply that tying access is impaired nor so shallow that the hook may shift under tying pressure. Tighten your vise's jaws firmly.

## Mounting The Hook In Your Vise— Problems, Solutions, And Suggestions

1. Don't try to hide the hook's point in your vise's jaws—this severely limits tying access.

## Starting The Thread

To start the thread, take up the bobbin in your right hand (remember, left-handers must trade left for right and vice versa). With your left hand, pull about a foot of thread off the bobbin. Above the hook, position the bobbin away from you and the thread end near you. Bring both hands down until the thread touches the hook's shank about 1/8 inch behind the eye. Now hold the thread end stationary as you orbit the bobbin around the hook's shank adding four turns of thread, each turn in front of the last, working toward the hook's eye. (Remember, the bobbin goes away from you when passing over the hook and toward you when passing under.) Wrap rearward (toward the hook's bend) in six consecutive thread turns; with that the thread should be firmly locked in place. Trim off the thread's end with your scissors' tips.

## Starting The Thread— Problems, Solutions, And Suggestions

1. If your lock knot keeps slipping as you form it, then you are probably not holding the thread end stationary, or else you are not using enough thread tension.

2. This is a good point at which to follow author-angler Dave Hughes' suggestion to intentionally break and then restart the thread on the hook several times—an excellent way in which to adjust your touch to just short of the thread's breaking point; this will insure that your flies are tight and durable.

**4.** Smash down the hook's barb.

**5.** On the left, a barb before smashing; on the right, a barb properly smashed.

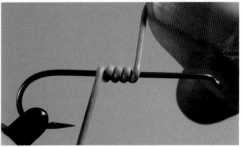
**6.** Starting the thread lock knot (fly line is shown instead of thread to best illustrate the process).

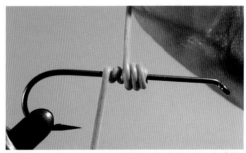
**7.** The lock knot completed. Trim the locked end of the thread.

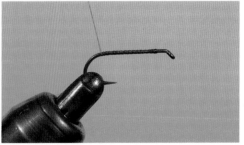
**8.** Spiral the thread back to the bend.

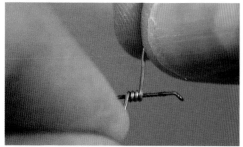

**9.** Wrap a layer of lead over the hook's shank.

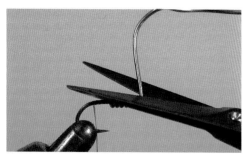

**10.** Trim closely the ends of the lead, but don't use your scissors' tips for this.

**11.** Press down the cut ends of the lead.

**12.** Secure the lead with tight thread turns.

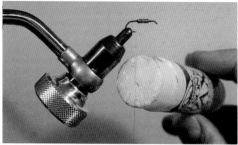

**13.** Waxing the thread is optional.

## Adding Lead

Spiral the thread back to the hook's bend (the point where the straight shank and bend meet) and let your bobbin hang. Break off a piece of lead about 5 inches long (or much longer if you plan to tie several Rick's Caddises, as there is less wasted lead this way). Hold the lead over the hook, one hand holding each end. Lower the lead so that it touches the hook about 1/8 inch in front of the bend (where the straight shank meets the bend); your left hand should be on the near side of the hook and your right hand on the far side. Move your left hand up against the hook. Hold your left hand stationary as you wrap the lead forward up the hook in close turns with your right hand (remember: away above the hook and toward you beneath); stop when the lead is about 1/8 inch behind the eye. Trim both ends of the lead closely using either your scissors, cutting deep into the blades and avoiding the tips, or with fingernail clippers. Press the cut ends of the lead firmly down with your finger or thumb nail or the flats of your scissor blades.

Wrap the thread forward over the lead in wide spirals—anything less than wide spirals tends to stall the thread in between two turns of lead resulting in repeated thread turns all in one place. When you reach the front of the lead, add a few tight thread turns right up against it to insure that it will never creep forward; then spiral the thread back to the bend.

## Adding Lead— Problems, Solutions, And Suggestions

1. Crowding the front of the hook with anything—fur, feathers, lead—creates problems when you later complete the fly with a thread head, so leave plenty of space between the front of the lead and the hook's eye.

2. Sometimes lead is crumbly and fragile. Your best chance to avoid breaking it is to slide your grip down the lead as you wrap it—this avoids fatiguing one spot on the lead.

## Dubbing The Abdomen

"Abdomen" refers to the rear portion of a fly, which may constitute half or more of the completed fly. This abdomen will be dubbed with fur (also called "dubbing").

You can dub without dubbing wax, but wax helps. Draw a few inches of thread from your bobbin. If you have dubbing wax, give the thread a light coating by sliding the wax down it. (Soft waxes will require only one or two light strokes; hard waxes may require more strokes and pressure.) Hold the bobbin in your left hand's second, third, and fourth fingers, and hold a ball of dubbing between the thumb and first finger of that hand. The dubbing shown is poly dubbing, but any green dubbing will do—rabbit, angora goat, squirrel, etc.

Draw a small amount of the dubbing from the ball with the thumb and first finger of your right hand. Spin the dubbing around the thread with the right-hand thumb and finger. The way I do this is to press the dubbing against the thread with the finger, and then slide the thumb and finger across one another. Continue spinning until the dubbing lays in a neat layer over the thread—this will only work if the dubbing is spun in one direction, as reversing directions merely unwraps the dubbing you've wrapped. Continue adding dubbing, slightly heavier each time, until it covers about 3 inches of thread. There will be a bit of bare thread between the dubbing and the hook; to get the dubbing to the hook, you can either slide the dubbing down the thread, or add thread turns until the bare thread is gone; either way is fine as long as the dubbing starts at the bend.

Wrap the dubbing forward (toward the eye) in close turns. You may have to add a couple of extra turns against the end of the lead to allow the dubbed thread to progress smoothly. Continue dubbing until you have covered about 2/3 to 3/4 of the shank. (The exact amount is not critical; the point is that this fly is composed mostly of abdomen.) Add more dubbing to the thread if necessary.

## Dubbing The Abdomen — Problems, Solutions, And Suggestions

1. The trick is to use enough dubbing to completely cover the lead and smooth out the abdomen without making it too bulky. Study the photos and practice. Most tiers try to spin far too much dubbing onto the thread; in most cases, almost any dubbing at all is plenty.

2. For a smoothly dubbed abdomen add the dubbing to the thread evenly, a little at a time.

3. The dubbing you draw from the ball will tend to pull away with most of its fibers aligned; try to spin these fibers at a right angle to the thread as you spin them on, this will really secure them.

4. Don't hesitate to back the dubbing over itself if necessary to cover lead or build a thin spot; dubbing is one of the few materials you can do this with and still get good results.

5. Give the completed abdomen a last inspection for exposed lead; if you find any, cover it with dubbing.

6. If the lead spreads out as you dub over it, it probably was secured inadequately, especially on the ends. To correct loose lead at this stage, run the thread quickly to the front of the lead and add a few tight turns there to stop the spreading; then add more tight thread turns back over the rest of the exposed lead.

## Dubbing The Thorax

"Thorax" refers to the section of a fly that is immediately behind the eye—in other words, the fly's "chest." Add dubbing to the thread as before, but use brown dubbing this time and add it a bit heavier than before (again, poly dubbing is shown here, but almost any fur can be used). Cover the lead and the shank between the abdomen and the eye with dubbing, but leave about 1/16 inch of bare shank behind the eye; here you will build a thread head.

## Dubbing The Thorax — Problems, Solutions, And Suggestions

1. As with the abdomen, check the thorax for exposed lead and if you find any, cover it with dubbing.

## Creating A Thread Head

Moisten your left-hand fingertips, and then use them to stroke back any dubbing fibers around the bare shank just behind the eye. Build a small, neat thread head that tapers from small at the eye to larger at the thorax.

## Creating A Thread Head — Problems, Solutions, And Suggestions

1. Work the thread gradually from the head's front to back. Steep thread angles and wide spirals make a head sloppy and insecure, so build the head with thread turns that are close and neat.

2. Remember to wrap the thread tightly for a sound head.

3. If you failed to leave the 1/16 inch of bare shank behind the eye, you will have demonstrated to yourself the value of this rule: Leaving plenty of room behind the eye insures neat and easy-to-execute thread heads.

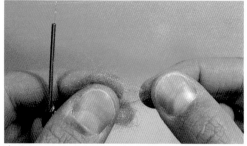
**14.** From a ball of dubbing, draw off a small amount.

**15.** Spin the dubbing onto the thread.

**16.** Dub the abdomen with green dubbing.

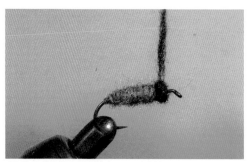
**17.** Dub the thorax with brown dubbing.

**18.** Moisten and stroke back the dubbing fibers from the eye, and then build a thread head.

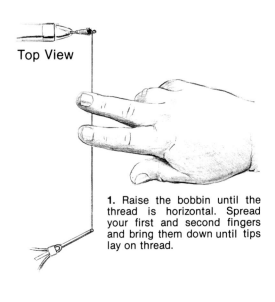

Top View

1. Raise the bobbin until the thread is horizontal. Spread your first and second fingers and bring them down until tips lay on thread.

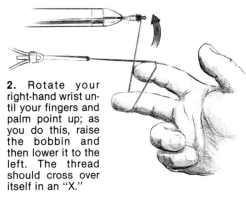

2. Rotate your right-hand wrist until your fingers and palm point up; as you do this, raise the bobbin and then lower it to the left. The thread should cross over itself in an "X."

3. Hook the far side of loop over the head.

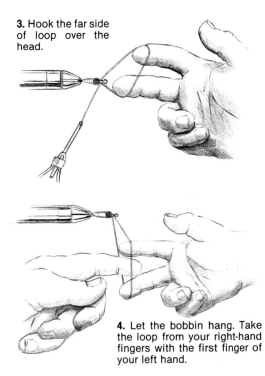

4. Let the bobbin hang. Take the loop from your right-hand fingers with the first finger of your left hand.

# The Half Hitch

A series of three consecutive half hitches will allow you to trim the thread end at the head and then complete the fly with a drop of head cement. Here is how to execute the half hitch.

Begin with the thread coming from the rear of the head. Release enough thread so that there is about 7 inches between the bobbin and the hook. Hold the bobbin in your left hand and bring it up toward you until it is level with the hook; only light tension need be applied to the thread. Extend the first and second fingers of your right hand and separate them about 1 inch. Bring the tips of your spread right-hand fingers down onto the thread; the palm of your right hand should be down. Now rotate and drop the wrist of your right hand until your right-hand's two fingers point up; as you do this, raise the bobbin and then bring it back down to the left until it is again level with the hook and the thread crosses itself in an "X." At this point, the right-hand fingers should be pointing up and should be inside a loop of thread; the left hand, and the bobbin, should be to the left and level with the hook. In essence, you have already formed the half hitch; all that remains is to get it onto the fly's head and tightened.

Hook one side of the half-hitch loop over the fly's head. Hold the loop over the fly and then catch the loop with the first finger of the left hand; it is easiest to catch the loop *between* the two right-hand fingers. Slip your right-hand fingers out of the loop; with your right hand, pick up something to guide the loop as it closes: scissors, a needle, bodkin, or hat pin. Use this object to take the loop from the left-hand finger. Draw the bobbin down or toward you with your left hand as you guide the loop closed with the object in your right. You have completed a half hitch (probably with considerable relief). Cut the thread closely.

Here is the good news and the bad news, the bad first: You must now add two more half hitches; the good news is that with repetition, half hitches get easier—quickly.

# The Half Hitch— Problems, Solutions, And Suggestions

1. Keep the half-hitch loop large, and be sure that it doesn't close as you work; a large loop makes execution of the half hitch much smoother and easier than does a small one.

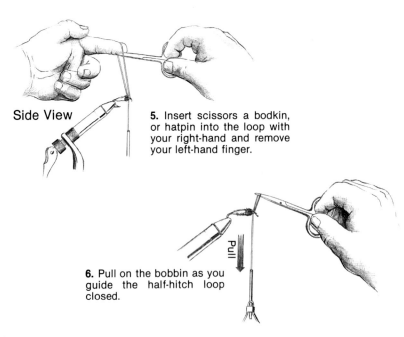

Side View

5. Insert scissors a bodkin, or hatpin into the loop with your right-hand and remove your left-hand finger.

6. Pull on the bobbin as you guide the half-hitch loop closed.

2. Remember to keep the loop on the *near* side of the hook until the ends of the loop cross in an "X"; once this is done, you can hook the loop over the fly's head.

3. Scissor blades will usually do a good job of guiding the half-hitch loop closed, but some scissors have rough surfaces on the outsides of the blades which will fray or cut the thread; if so, use a hat pin or bodkin instead.

4. The reason for holding the half-hitch loop *above* the hook is because the down eye insures that the loop will not slip loose of the hook; on up-eye hooks, hold the loop *beneath* the hook.

5. Whatever you use to guide the half-hitch loop closed, get the loop well up it to start with; just before the loop closes, slide the object out.

6. Light tension on the closing loop maintains control; heavy tension is awkward and unnecessary; no tension offers no control.

7. The angle of the object guiding the loop determines whether the loop slides up or down the object or stays put.

## Cementing The Head

To really secure a fly head you will need to coat it with "head cement,"; head cement is anything that will effectively do the securing—glue, varnish, lacquer. Fly shops carry head cements, and you can probably find a variety of other products that will work well. My favorite is a two-part rod builder's epoxy glue called Crystal Clear Epoxy; it is made by the Epoxy Coatings Company. It is tough and seems to have no harmful or unpleasant vapors, but it takes a few hours to cure, and because it is so tough it's difficult to remove if it ends up in the wrong places. It is my first choice because it makes a fly head durable and handsome.

Regardless of what head cement you choose, application is the same: With a pointed object—a bodkin, needle, or round toothpick—dab a dot of cement onto the head and then spread it over the entire thread head. Add more cement as needed; one thin coating is usually sufficient. Set the fly aside until the head cement is fully hardened (sticking the fly horizontally into a block of wood works well).

## Cementing The Head—
## Problems, Solutions, And Suggestions

1. Thin head cements can be deceptive because they tend to saturate rather than build—the tier keeps adding cement to create a smooth, glossy head, but the cement simply soaks throughout the fly's materials sapping their vibrancy. Two or more coatings, each allowed to solidify (at least partially) before the next is applied are the best way to build with thin head cements, although one coat is usually all that is really necessary.

2. It is a good idea to check your flies a few minutes after applying head cement to make certain that it has not seeped into and filled the hook eye. If this happens the cement will still be soft enough so that you can clear it from the eye with a thick hackle stem or the sharp point of a round toothpick.

3. For efficiency, coat the heads of several flies at once rather than head cementing each fly before tying another.

We have covered a lot of ground with the Rick's Caddis—many of the really essential techniques and concepts of fly tying. From here we can build a step at a time; we will not need to move so rapidly. But you have come this far, and you have gained valuable knowledge, skills, and understanding. Let's build on them.

**19.** Create a half-hitch loop and hook it over the thread head.

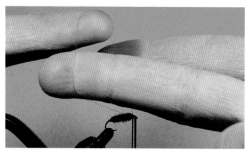
**20.** Pass the half-hitch loop to the first finger on your left hand.

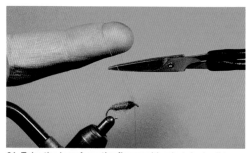
**21.** Take the loop from the finger with a hatpin, bodkin, or your scissors' tips.

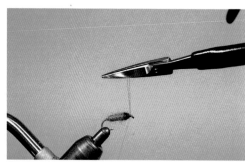
**22.** Guide the loop closed.

**23.** Add head cement.

# WHITE AND GRIZZLY WOOLLY BUGGER

The terrifically popular Woolly Bugger is the close cousin of the old standby Woolly Worm. Both flies are tied in nearly the same fashion and both are extremely productive and versatile.

In tying the Woolly Bugger you will learn to work with marabou, chenille, and hackle—hackle, and the techniques for selecting, sizing, and winding it, will be a recurring subject throughout this book.

The Woolly Bugger can be tied weighted or unweighted. It is usually fished with a pulsing swimming motion from deep to shallow in streams or lakes. This fly, that will take trout, char, Atlantic salmon, steelhead, bass, and saltwater species, is indeed versatile.

The Woolly Bugger originated in the vise of Russell Blessing.

## WHITE AND GRIZZLY WOOLLY BUGGER

**Hook:** 4X long, regular to heavy wire, sizes 2 to 14.
**Thread:** 3/0 for sizes 8 and up; 6/0 or 8/0 for sizes 10 down, white (although variations may call for other colors).
**Tail:** White marabou (other more natural colors may be substituted).
**Hackle:** Grizzly (but almost any color can be used).
**Body:** White chenille (variations include a variety of other colors) large-diameter for sizes 6 and up; medium-diameter for sizes 8 and down.

## Selecting The Hackle

A saddle hackle with soft fibers is my first choice for a Woolly Bugger, but a large dry-fly neck hackle is usually soft enough to do a good job. Sizing hackles with a hackle gauge is easy— just use a hackle that your gauge indicates is appropriate for your hook size (in this case, size 6). If you lack a gauge, wrap hackles around the hook until you find one with fibers about 1 1/2 to 2 times as long as the width of the hook's gape (the "gape" is the space between the hook's point and shank); this last method must be performed after the hook is mounted in your vise.

**1.** Sizing a hackle with a hackle gauge.

## Selecting The Hackle— Problems, Solutions, And Suggestions

1. Most hackles have longer fibers at the butt than at the tip—so, by which fibers should the hackle be gauged? My solution is to gauge a hackle by its longest, or nearly longest, fibers, and this seems to produce the best proportions.

## Preparing The Tail

Smash the barb on a 4X long size-6 medium- to heavy-wire hook, and mount the hook firmly in your vise (the hook shown is a Tiemco model 9395). Start the thread in the center of the shank, and then spiral it to the bend. Select a full, soft marabou plume. Wet the plume by dipping your thumb and fingers in water and then stroking the plume (dry marabou is unruly; wet behaves). Measure the plume by holding it against the hook. To do this hold the plume just over the hook and parallel to its shank, set the tip of the plume at the bend, and note the point on the plume that is immediately above the front end of the shank—from this measured point, the plume is equal to the shank in length and this is the part of plume that will project from the bend.

## The Pinch And Adding The Tail

Hold the plume on top of the shank at the hook's bend between the thumb and first finger of your left hand. The tips of the plume should now project off the hook's bend, and your thumb and finger should be holding the butts of the plume (at the shank-length point on the plume that you noted earlier when measuring) right over the thread end. Now it is time to execute a technique that I have always called the "pinch." (I was surprised to discover that fly tier-author Dick Talleur also calls it the pinch—the name is obviously appropriate.) The pinch is a method for controlling soft materials as they are secured under thread turns—we will use the pinch throughout this book.

Bring the bobbin toward you and then straight up over the hook while maintaining constant, firm thread tension. Move your left hand back slightly (left-handers substitute "right" for "left" and vice versa: last reminder). Don't slide the thumb and finger back; instead, roll back their tips as you draw the joints closer together—this will open wider the space between the thumb and finger tips. Move the bobbin rearwards (in the direction of the hook's bend: last reminder) bringing the thread back between your thumb's tip and the marabou plume; keep bringing the thread back until it nestles securely in this spot. With only slight tension on the thread (it should stay locked between the thumb and plume), bring the bobbin down and back along the far side of the hook as you guide the thread in between the plume and your *fingertip*. You now have a loop of thread around the plume. Move your left hand slightly forward as you roll your thumb and finger tips together and widen the space between their joints— your thumb and finger tips should now enclose the loop of thread. Hold the plume firmly as you close the thread loop by pulling firmly down and slightly toward you on the bobbin. By executing the pinch, you have managed to secure a soft material (a marabou plume) while controlling its position—congratulations!

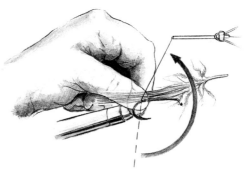

**1.** Hold the material to shank. Raise the bobbin.

**2.** Bring the joints of your thumb and finger closer together; this will spread apart your thumbtip from your fingertip; slip the thread back between thumbtip and material.

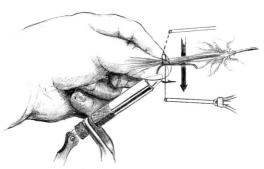

**3.** Bring the thread (and bobbin) down the far side of the material as you draw the thread back between fingertip and material.

**4.** Widen the gap between your thumb and finger joints closing thumbtip and fingertip around loop.

**5.** Pull down on the bobbin, tightening the pinch loop.

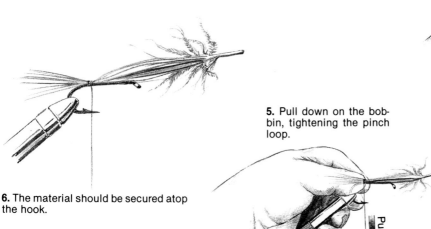

**6.** The material should be secured atop the hook.

Pull

**2.** Sizing a hackle by wrapping it around the shank.

**3.** A single marabou plume.

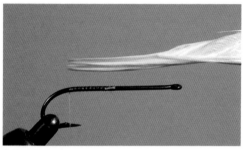

**4.** Wet and then measure the marabou plume.

**5.** Tie in the marabou plume using the pinch. Add four securing thread turns over the pinch turn; then lift the butt of the plume and spiral the thread forward.

**6.** Lower the plume's butt and tie it in using the pinch. Lift the plume's butt and snip it closely; then spiral the thread down to the bend.

## The Pinch And Adding The Tail— Problems, Solutions, And Suggestions

1. Remember to use *slight* tension on the thread as you form the pinch loop—no tension sacrifices control; firm tension closes the loop too soon. This regards the *forming* of the pinch loop; the *tightening* of the pinch loop will require lots of thread tension.

2. Make sure the material to be secured (in this case, a marabou plume) is right down against the hook, otherwise the thread loop will tend to slide down the front of the material. You may need to slide your thumb and finger tips down over the hook's shank a bit to accomplish this.

3. Once you have tightened the pinch loop of thread, allow no slack until you have really locked the pinch in with additional tight turns (next step), otherwise the tails are likely to shift or rotate around the hook—exactly the kind of problem a well-executed pinch should eliminate.

## Completing The Tail

Add four tight securing thread turns over the pinch turn. Lift the butt end of the plume with your left hand, and spiral the thread up the shank to a point 1/8 inch behind the eye with your right. Lower the plume's butt to the shank and tie it in at the 1/8 inch point using the pinch. Add four tight securing thread turns over the pinch turn. Lift the remainder of the butts and trim them closely. Spiral the thread down the marabou-covered shank to the bend. With that your Woolly Bugger's tail is complete.

## Completing The Tail— Problems, Solutions, And Suggestions

1. There will probably be leftover marabou fibers at the base of the plume that are too short or too far from the tip to end up in the tail. These are some of the softest fibers and really come alive in the water. Strip them and bunch them for the next Woolly Bugger tail—or add them to the tip for a tail that is really thick.

## Tying In The Hackle

Strip the fuzzy fibers from both sides of the hackle's stem at its base. Hold the hackle to the hook with your left hand; its stem should be in line with the shank, hackle butt forward and tip extending off the bend; the bare stem should end, and the fibers begin, right at the bend. Using the pinch, tie in the hackle and then add four tight thread turns. Lift the stem and spiral the thread up the shank to a point about 1/8 inch behind the hook's eye; lower the stem to the shank and tie it down using the pinch; then secure it with four tight thread turns and lift the stem and trim it closely.

## Tying In The Hackle— Problems, Solutions, And Suggestions

1. Make sure that the thread turns that secure the hackle are no farther back than the ones that secure the tail because if they are, the hackle thread turns might kick the tails out of position. This is a good rule to follow whenever you are working near the bend: After each material is secured under thread turns, the thread should never again travel back beyond those turns.

2. If you strip the hackle's stem completely, not only partially, you will eliminate the chance of any fuzz getting in your way when securing the stem near the hook's eye.

3. If you leave a little bare stem showing at the tie-in point at the bend, you'll have insurance that your hackle will lay neatly when it is later wrapped.

## Tying In And Wrapping The Chenille

For the No. 6 hook you will want to use the chenille designated as "large." Snip off about a 7 inch length of chenille. In a few turns, work the thread back another 1/16 inch from the eye (total distance from the eye should now be about 3/16 inch). Secure the end of the chenille at this point using the pinch; a stub of about 1/2 inch should now project from the front of the tie-in point. Add four more tight thread turns at the tie-in point, and then snip closely the chenille's stub end. Hold the chenille under tension at a slight angle above the shank as you spiral the thread down both to the bend. Add four more tight thread turns at the bend. Spiral the thread forward to a point about 1/8 inch behind the eye.

Pass the chenille from hand to hand as you wrap it in close, tight turns up the shank. When it reaches the hanging thread, hold the end of the chenille up and forward in your right hand, pass the bobbin (and, of course, the thread) just in front of the wrapped chenille and over the chenille's end, lower the bobbin down the far side of the hook and let it hang. Regrasp the bobbin in your left hand from the near side of the hook and draw the thread tight. This locks the chenille in place. Release the chenille's end and take up the bobbin in your right hand and add four tight securing turns of thread. Snip off the chenille's end closely with your scissor's tips.

## Tying In The Chenille — Problems, Solutions, And Suggestions

1. If the tail spins around the shank as you secure the chenille at the bend, it is probably due to one of the following: The thread turns you made at the bend for the tail, hackle, or both are too loose (you can fix this by holding everything in place and making tight turns when you secure the chenille at the bend), or you wrapped the thread back too far when securing the chenille at the bend (this can be cured by simply un-wrapping those turns and then adding them a bit farther forward at, or slightly forward of, the turns securing the tail). (See "Tying In The Hackle"—Problems, Solutions, and Suggestions.)

## Wrapping The Hackle

Your next step will be to spiral the hackle up the chenille body; wrapping a hackle in spaced turns is called "palmering" a hackle. Squeeze your hackle pliers at their center until their jaws open; then close them on the tip of the hackle. Be certain the jaws are locked onto the stem as well as the fibers. Insert the first finger of your right hand into the loop at the end of the pliers (some hackle pliers don't have a loop so in this case, simply hold the pliers by the end opposite the jaws). As you palmer the hackle up the chenille body, you will have to pass the pliers to your left hand each time they go beneath the hook and then bring the right around to reinsert your finger into the plier's loop—the hanging thread makes continuous wrapping with the right hand impossible. Keep constant, moderate pressure on the hackle as you palmer it up the body to the hook's eye in five to seven turns.

As you hold the hackle's tip up and leaning forward off the hook's eye with your right hand, bring the thread up over the hackle's stem with your left, and then lower the bobbin down the far side of the hook—now you have secured the hackle's tip in the same manner in which you secured the chenille's end. Continue holding the hackle pliers stationary in your right hand as you work three more thread turns onto the same spot. Let the bobbin hang as you squeeze the hackle pliers until their jaws open; release the hackle's tip and set the pliers aside. Add two tight thread turns and closely trim off the hackle's tip.

**7.** Strip the fibers from the hackle's stem at its base.

**8.** A properly stripped hackle and one that is not yet stripped.

**9.** Tie in the hackle using the pinch; then add four securing thread turns over the pinch turn. Lift the hackle's stem and spiral the thread forward. Lower the stem and secure it with the pinch and a few securing thread turns as you did with the plume's butt. Lift and snip the stem.

**10.** Using the pinch, tie in the chenille, add securing thread turns. Spiral the thread down the chenille to the bend, and then trim closely the chenille's stub end.

**11.** Spiral the thread forward. Wrap the chenille up the shank in close, tight turns. Secure the chenille's end with thread; then trim the chenille's stub end.

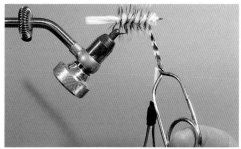

**12.** Palmer the hackle up the chenille body. Wrap the hackle with your finger in the loop of your hackle pliers.

**13.** Tie off the hackle just behind the hook's eye.

**14.** Trim the hackle's tip closely.

**15.** Finger position for the triangle. Note the tiny space in the center.

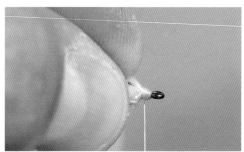

**16.** Clear the head area using the triangle. Create a thread head. Notice how the triangle allows clear access.

# Wrapping The Hackle—
# Problems, Solutions, And Suggestions

1. The safest way to mount the hackle's tip in the plier's jaws is with the stem in line with the pliers, because an angled stem can weaken and then break once tension is applied to it.

2. Keep the pliers in line with the stem as you palmer the hackle for the same reason as No. 1.

3. It is best to get the plier's jaws well up the hackle's tip, say 1/2 inch, because the point of a hackle is fragile, and it is beyond the part of the feather that should be palmered over the body anyway.

4. Hackles have a limit as to how much tension they can stand; this is considerably less than chenille's limit. Develop a sense of how much tension each material can handle, for hackles or anything else.

5. If your hackle breaks as you palmer it, it will probably break right at your plier's jaws; if that happens, regrasp what's left of the hackle in your pliers and start palmering again from the beginning. Add less turns of hackle if necessary.

6. The spacing of the hackle turns will be determined by the angle of the hackle to the hook as the hackle is wrapped—if the angle varies, so will the spacing of the turns; if the angle is steep, the turns will be widely spread; if the angle is minor, the turns will be close. All this is equally true of anything wrapped on a hook.

# The Triangle

Forming a neat thread head on the Woolly Bugger requires one more step than does the thread head on the Rick's Caddis. To get stray hackle fibers and chenille fuzz back out of the way for the forming of this head, I use a technique I call the "triangle."

Begin the triangle by bringing together the tips of the thumb, first finger, and second finger of your left hand; viewing the tips from the front will reveal within them a tiny, three-cornered opening for which this procedure was named. Hold the bobbin under moderate tension in your right hand as you slip the triangle opening over the hook's eye. Lower the heel of your left hand until the hand is cupped around the fly. Draw your left hand back and, as you do, the hackle fibers and chenille fuzz around the eye will draw back also. Squeeze your left-hand thumb and finger tips together as you draw back the materials, but allow the thread end to pass between the tips of your thumb and second finger.

Now you have full access to the head area behind the eye. Add thread turns until you have covered completely the trimmed ends of all materials—in this case, chenille and hackle. If the thread has formed a neat, conical shape, tapering from small at the eye to larger at the front of the chenille body, stop; if not, continue adding thread until it does. With that, the basic thread head is complete. Add three half hitches, trim the thread, and add head cement.

# The Triangle—
# Problems, Solutions, And Suggestions

1. Even pressure from your thumb and fingertips helps make the triangle work smoothly, so check to make certain that none of the three is applying more or less pressure than any other.

2. Before sliding back your hand during execution of the pinch, be certain that the heel of your left hand is well down below the hook, because if the left hand is too high, the pinch becomes awkward.

3. Keep your thumb and two fingers well bent so their tips do the work.

4. Draw the hackles and chenille fibers back only as far as is needed to clear the head area—the farther you draw them back, the more likely it is that the materials you are trying to control will escape.

# GOLD RIBBED HARE'S EAR

There are few flies that rival the Gold Ribbed Hare's Ear in popularity. This scruffy, simple nymph has proven consistently attractive to trout and anglers everywhere, and it can be tied quickly and easily. There are numerous variations, but the pattern listed here is quite standard.

The Gold Ribbed Hare's Ear can be swum from deep to shallow in streams or lakes, or fished dead drift in streams. While it is generally weighted with a few turns of lead under the thorax, unweighted versions are usually best for fishing near the surface.

Here you will have more opportunity to practice dubbing; you will also rib with oval gold tinsel, and create a wing case—both techniques are valuable and used frequently.

## GOLD RIBBED HARE'S EAR

**Hook:** Any heavy wire hook 2X, 1X, or standard length, size 18 to 8.
**Thread:** Black, 6/0 or 8/0.
**Weight:** For hook sizes 14 and larger, No. 2 lead; for sizes 16 and smaller, No. 1.
**Tail:** Guard hairs from hare's mask.
**Rib:** Fine oval gold tinsel.
**Abdomen:** Hare's mask.
**Wing Case:** Brown mottled turkey-quill section.
**Thorax:** Hare's mask.

## Adding The Lead

Smash down the barb on a size-12 heavy wire 1X or 2X long hook and mount it in your vise (the hook shown is a Daiichi model No. 1550). Start the thread about 1/16 inch behind the eye and spiral it back to just past the center of the shank. Wrap No. 2 lead from the center of the shank and stop just short of the 1/16 inch gap behind the eye (this will probably require only three or four turns of lead). Secure the lead under tight thread turns and then spiral the thread back to the bend.

## Adding The Lead—
## Problems, Solutions, And Suggestions

1. See "Adding the lead—problems, solutions, and suggestions" for the Green Caddis Larva.

## Tying In The Tail

Although I have seen a number of variations, the tails I see most often on the Gold Ribbed Hare's Ear (which is often referred to simply as

**1.** Start the thread, add lead, secure the lead with thread turns, work the thread back to the bend.

**2.** Snip some fur from a hare's mask for a tail (or use a substitute).

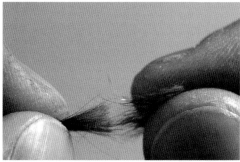

**3.** Stroke most of the fuzz away leaving mostly guard hair.

**4.** Measure the tuft of hair against the hook, tie in the tuft at the bend using the pinch, and add securing thread turns. Lift the butts of the tuft, advance the thread, and tie in the butts using the pinch.

**5.** Tie in the end of the tinsel using the light turn. Lift the tinsel and spiral the thread down it to the bend. Add tight securing thread turns.

the "Hare's Ear") are hare's mask guard hairs. This requires that you purchase a hare's mask instead of simply purchasing a bag of pre-blended hare's mask fur—the pre-blended fur is fine for all the dubbing of this fly but not for creating the tails. Since there are a lot of variations of this pattern, I think it is fine if you choose to substitute hackle fibers, partridge-feather fibers, grouse-feather fibers, pheasant-tail fibers, or anything acceptable in place of the hare's mask-guard hair tail. But if you do have a mask, here is how to use it.

In your left hand, grasp a small tuft of fur somewhere around the center of the mask and cut it loose close to the hide. Reposition this tuft so that you end up gripping it by its tips; hold the tips tightly between the thumb and first finger of your left hand. Draw out the short fibers by grasping the exposed part of the tuft (the butts) between the thumb and first finger of your right hand and maintaining modest pressure as you pull that hand away; only the "guard hairs," the long, substantial hairs that project beyond the soft underfur, and a bit of underfur remain. Measure the hairs and note the point at which they are about one half to two thirds the hook's total length, and then tie them in at the bend using the pinch. Lift the butts of the tail fibers and advance the thread to just short of the lead. Bring the butts back down and tie them in using the pinch. Add some tight securing thread turns. Trim the butts of the fibers closely if necessary (the butts of the guard hairs may not reach the lead).

## Tying In The Tail— Problems, Solutions, And Suggestions

1. Bear in mind that the natural insect imitated by the Gold Ribbed Hare's Ear has only two or three tails; the hair tail you tie in will have much more than two or three fibers—just avoid the impression of a brush.

2. Don't worry about getting all the underfur out of the guard hairs, this is unnecessary and time consuming.

## The Light Turn And Tying In The Oval Gold Tinsel

There are two ways to deal with the oval gold tinsel: You can cut off a piece about 3 inches long, or you can simply unravel some from the spool and set the spool on the table to the rear of the fly. The latter helps hold the tinsel out of your way and seems most efficient.

The light-tension thread turn, which I simply refer to as the "light turn," is a handy alternate technique to the pinch and is a bit quicker for tying in stiff materials. To execute the light turn, hold the gold tinsel near its end; if the end is frayed, trim it clean. Hold the end of the gold tinsel down along the shank with its end slightly to your side of the hook and right up against the rear of the lead. Bring the thread up and over the end of the tinsel—use only *light* tension on the thread. Draw the bobbin down to close the thread loop; as you do this, the gold tinsel will roll right up on top of the shank—and there is no end to trim. Add a few tight securing thread turns. Hold the tinsel back and slightly above the shank as you spiral the thread down it to the bend; add a few tight turns here too.

## The Light Turn And Tying In The Gold Rope—Problems, Solutions, And Suggestions

1. If the gold tinsel keeps slipping out of position, grasp it after the thread loop is in place as though you were finishing a pinch. Eventually you will be able to efficiently perform the light turn without this.

2. Don't confuse light tension with no tension or moderate tension—no tension offers no control, whereas even moderate tension will roll the tinsel around the shank ahead of the thread.

3. A last reminder: never wrap the thread back farther than the securing wraps for the tail.

## Dubbing And Ribbing The Abdomen

The fur used for dubbing a Gold Ribbed Hare's Ear comes from a hare's mask. You can purchase a hare's mask and blend the fur yourself, or you can take the easy route and purchase it pre-blended; as I mentioned before, the only drawback in buying the pre-blended fur is that you will have to substitute another tail for the usual hare's mask-guard hair tail (but this substitution, as previously mentioned, is fine).

If you have a hare's mask, here is how its fur is prepared and blended. Begin by closely snipping the fur from the areas shown in the illustration. Remember to leave a bit of this fur on the hide for making tails. Because the fur from different parts of the mask will vary in character, blending is in order. Here is how to blend by hand: Take a clump of fur, pull it in half, lay one half over the other, pull the resulting clump in half again, and repeat this sequence until you are satisfied that the blending is adequate.

A more thorough method involves a household electric blender: Just toss in the fur and some water and blend briefly on low. Once blended, remove all the fur, squeeze it between paper towels, remove it, and allow it to dry. Another answer is the little blenders offered through fly shops specifically for blending furs; they blend without water, making the process neat and quick.

Whether your fur was pre-blended or not, it is time to dub the abdomen. Wax the thread if you wish, and then spin a layer of fur onto it. Dub from the bend up to about the second turn of lead, a bit more than halfway up the shank. Attempt to create a tapered abdomen—fine at the bend and thicker at the thorax area.

If you left the rope on its spool, trim it now, about 3 inches from the fly. Spiral the gold rope forward up the abdomen in five or six turns; the turns, "ribs," may be evenly spaced or may widen slightly as they progress. Tie off the rope at the end of the dubbed abdomen, add a few securing thread turns, and trim the end of the rope deep into your scissor's blades.

## Dubbing And Ribbing The Abdomen— Problems, Solutions, And Suggestions

1. Make certain that you dub *past* the center of the shank; this is good insurance that there will be no exposed lead after the next few steps.

2. See "dubbing the abdomen" for the Rick's Caddis.

3. Although firm tension while wrapping the gold rope is desirable, extreme tension can kick the tail over even if it is well secured. If the tail kicks over without extreme tension, use as much tension as possible and better secure the tail next time.

4. While ribbing, watch the angle of the gold rope between the fly and your hand—if the angle is constant, the spacing of the ribs will be constant; also, a steep angle will produce widely spaced ribs, while a slight angle will space them closely. Steadily increasing the steepness of this angle will produce ribs that steadily widen.

## Tying In The Turkey Section And Dubbing The Thorax

Cut a section about 3/16 inches wide from a turkey quill feather; cut close to the quill (be warned that the term "quill" may refer to a whole wing or tail feather, the hollow, horny stem of such a feather, or even the individual fibers of a feather. This may seem confusing, but the context usually makes the usage clear). Roll this section around the top half of

**HARE'S MASK**

Trim fur from shaded area.

**6.** Dub a tapered abdomen to just past midshank with the fur from a hare's mask.

**7.** Spiral the tinsel up the abdomen; then secure the tinsel with thread wraps and trim the tinsel's end.

**8.** Snip a section from a brown mottled turkey quill.

**9.** Roll the section around the lead, and then tie in the section with a modified pinch. Add several tight securing thread turns.

**10.** Snip the end of the turkey section; dub the thorax heavily.

**11.** Draw the turkey section forward flatly and secure it with a turn of thread.

**12.** After trimming the turkey section, building a thread head, and adding three half hitches, pick out some fibers at the sides of the thorax, and add head cement.

the lead; the butts of the section should extend forward no farther than the eye, and the tips of the section should extend rearward. Make a light turn over the section, and then roll the first finger and thumb of your left hand over the section and the thread in a sort of modified pinch; try to spread this pinch out over both sides of the section. Pull the thread tight; then add a few securing turns. Trim the end of the turkey section.

Add dubbing to the thread a bit heavier than usual. Dub heavily from the point where the turkey section is tied in, forward to just behind the eye, but do leave space behind the eye for a thread head.

## Tying In The Turkey Section And Dubbing The Thorax—Problems, Solutions, And Suggestions

1. Try to handle the cut turkey section carefully so as to maintain its shape; this will make it easiest to work with.

2. When tying in the turkey section, it helps to remember what you are trying to accomplish—to secure the section so that it doesn't bunch but instead rolls around the thorax neatly and flatly.

3. There will be a bright side and a dull side to the turkey; if you tie the bright side down, against the thorax, it will show when you complete the last tying steps. Bright side or dull side showing—it's a matter of personal taste.

4. Don't hesitate to dub slightly back over the abdomen in order to insure that the thread securing the turkey section is thoroughly covered with dubbing.

5. It helps smooth out the drop off at the end of the lead if you add a few extra turns of dubbing at that point.

6. For an unweighted Hare's Ear (which is a most useful version), remember to compensate for the missing lead by substantially building up the thorax.

## Creating The Wing Case

Pull the turkey section forward over the thorax with your right hand; then work the bobbin (and a turn of thread) over it with your left. Continue to hold the section under tension as you draw the thread tight with your left hand. Release the section from your right hand, and then switch the *bobbin* to your right hand without releasing the thread tension; then add a few tight securing turns. Trim the section closely, draw back any wild dubbing with the triangle, build a thread head, and secure it with three half hitches. To create the impression of legs, tease some fur and guard hairs out from both sides of the thorax with your scissor's tips, a bodkin, or a hat pin. Add head cement to the thread head to complete the Gold Ribbed Hare's Ear.

## Creating The Wing Case— Problems, Solutions, And Suggestions

1. For a neat, even wing case, pull the turkey section *flatly* over the thorax. Holding the turkey between the thumb and first finger with the thumb on top seems to work best.

2. At first, you might do best to leave plenty of head space behind the eye, and then trim the turkey section only moderately close; this may result in a large head, but if closely cut turkey fibers slip loose, they cannot be saved. As your skills improve you can work progressively closer.

3. If you do want close-cut turkey for a small head, lift the fibers under some tension and then snip close; snip around a few additional times to pare down the turkey stubs.

# MORRISTONE

The Morristone is the result of my several-year quest for a productive quick-to-tie soft-material stonefly nymph imitation. The tying procedure is a bit unconventional, but you will learn how to heavily weight a fly, work with yarn, create flat-feather legs and of course, how to tie another effective fly.

It seemed as though the Morristone's dressing was confirmed by divine intervention when a seven-pound steelhead took one and forced me a good quarter mile down river before the end of the struggle. Two days of successful trout fishing on the Deschutes River had convinced me that this pattern was durable and persuasive. I knew, of course, that the steelhead proved nothing, but how could the timing, the felicity, of it mean anything except that this fly was right by God and nature? With the big fish on the bank, I knelt and worked the fly free. Moments later, knee deep in a backwater, I held the fish gently upright until it bolted lightly from my hands. In that moment, with the sun on my back and the promise of a good riffle before me, I confirmed the final dressing of the Morristone and thought how clean, how ideal, had been its proving. A month later I found a better tail; I hope God and nature will understand.

The Morristone can be—and often is—weighted with only one layer of lead or none. But because it is generally fished along the bottom in fast, broken water—stonefly water—the double layer of lead makes sense. In a pinch I have used the Morristone to imitate insects other than the stonefly nymph; last August I fished it deep in a lake to suggest a big dragonfly nymph, and the rainbow trout took it steadily and faithfully. Generally, though, it is best fished dead drift and well down in fast currents.

## MORRISTONE

**Hook:** Heavy wire, 3X to 6X long, sizes 10 to 6.
**Thread:** Dark, 8/0, 6/0, or 3/0 (I recommend that you start with 3/0).
**Tail:** Brown, mottled hen-saddle tip with center removed.
**Abdomen And Thorax:** Dark gray yarn (I like Antron yarn).
**Rib:** Any brown rib—dyed monofilament, Swannendaze (thin), or dubbed thread as examples—but my favorite is V rib.
**Wing Case:** Pheasant-tail fibers, dark side showing.
**Legs:** Brown, mottled hen saddle feather (same feather as used for the tail).
**Head:** Dark brown dubbing.

Before we proceed, I'd like to explain the system, albeit loose and not always adhered to, used for listing fly patterns. The idea is to list a fly's components in the order in which the tier uses them. This helps clarify tying procedure, especially if specific instructions are sketchy or nonexistent. Many experienced tiers will adjust things to their own tying style anyway—adding weight after the tail is tied in rather than before as the pattern suggests and so on—but the order of materials can still add clarity.

It's a logical system, but it is far from perfect. The wing-case fibers for the Gold Ribbed Hare's Ear, for example, are tied in before the thorax is dubbed, but the wing case is really formed *after* the dubbing of the thorax—therefore, which should be listed first: the wing case, or the thorax? In the pattern for the Morristone, I have grouped the abdomen and thorax together, because they are both of gray yarn; to do so is logical and expedient, but it is arguably against the system's guidelines.

Despite these shortcomings, and the fact that through ignorance, absentmindedness, or choice it is sometimes ignored, the system for listing fly patterns makes sense and can be helpful.

**1.** Wrap a layer of lead onto the hook; then wrap a second layer over the first; the second layer should be shorter than the first. Measure and strip a hen-hackle feather.

**2.** Draw the fibers to the sides and snip off the tip.

**3.** Trim the fibers at the base of the tip as shown.

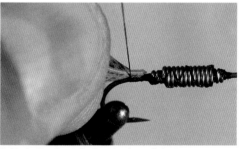

**4.** Tie in the tip at the bend using a light turn.

**5.** Tie in the V-rib and then the yarn.

## Adding The Double Layer Of Lead

Smash the barb on a size-8, heavy-wire, long-shank hook (the hook shown is a Partridge Grey Shadow, model No. GRS4A), and mount it in your vise. Start the thread about 3/16 inch behind the eye, and spiral it quickly to the bend. Wrap a layer of No. 2 lead from about 1/8 inch ahead of the bend to about 3/16 inch behind the eye, and then trim and press down the ends. Wrap a second layer of lead over the first; this second layer should be about three lead turns short of the first at each end. Bind the lead with thread turns.

You can, of course, tie the Morristone with only a single layer of lead. The finished Morristone shown at the beginning of this section has only one layer of lead.

## Adding The Double Layer Of Lead— Problems, Solutions, And Suggestions

1. Use only moderate tension when adding the second layer of lead, or it will spread out the first.

2. This long-shank hook will be more flexible than the hooks we have used previously, therefore you may need to support it occasionally throughout the tying of the Morristone (see "Essential Guidelines" No. 4 in the "White and Grizzly Woolly Bugger").

## Tying In The Tail, Rib, And Yarn

Select a brown, mottled hen-saddle feather, and pluck it from the neck. Measure it by holding the fibers along the shank; you are looking for fibers that are about 1/2 to 2/3 as long as the shank. Strip all the fibers that are longer than this from the stem, leaving it bare at its base. Draw at least 3/8 inch of fibers out to both sides of the stem; these fiber sections should start with the longest remaining fibers, those nearest the stem's base. Snip off the tip of the feather just above the side-drawn fiber sections. Set the body of the feather aside; it will be used later.

Take up the tip and snip the fibers off along both sides of the stem at its base; snip back about 1/8 inch. Hold the feather horizontally and lower its trimmed base to the top of the hook at its bend; the bulk of the feather should project off the bend, and the curve of the feather should sweep upward. Using a light turn, tie in the feather by its trimmed stem. Add several securing thread turns; try to keep the feather horizontal both from end to end and from side to side as you do this, although it can be off a bit and still produce a fly that is perfectly effective.

Again using a light turn, tie in one end of a section of V-rib at the rear of the lead, and then run the thread down the V-rib to the bend and add a few tight securing thread turns there.

Tie in the yarn up against the rear of the lead using the pinch. Run the thread down the yarn to the bend, and then add securing thread turns as you did with the V-rib. If necessary, trim the butts of the V-rib and yarn, and then bind the cut ends under turns of thread.

## Tying In The Tail, Rib, And Yarn— Problems, Solutions, And Suggestions

1. Before you snip the tip off the hen feather, be certain that you left *at least* 3/8 inches of fibers on the main part of the feather.

2. To allow for the pull of the thread, tie in the feather tipped slightly toward you; as a result, the feather will roll neatly into position.

3. In tying in the feather, use most of the 1/8 inch of trimmed stem; this will insure that it is securely fastened.

4. Don't try to save time by simply stripping the fibers from the tip's base—to do so will weaken the feather, and when you tie it in it may want to roll onto its side.

5. V-rib is stiff enough for the light turn, but barely, so you may have to hold the V-rib very near the tie-in point.

## Tying In The Wing Case Fibers And Legs

Advance your thread to just past the center of the shank. Cut about a 1/4 inch section of fibers from a pheasant tail; try to keep the section flat and intact. Tie in the section just forward of the center of the shank as you did the turkey section for the Gold Ribbed Hare's Ear; the dark side of the pheasant section should be down, bright side up.

Take up the cut hen hackle you set aside earlier. Draw forward the last 1/8 inch of fibers at the cut end of the stem, where the tip was. Hold these fibers with your right-hand thumb and finger as you draw the remaining fibers back between your left-hand thumb and first finger. Your thumb should be on top of the concave side of the feather (in other words, the feather's curve should be toward your thumb). Hold the left-hand fibers and release the others from your right hand; now the bulk of the fibers should be back neatly and securely gathered in your left hand with the 1/8 inch of fibers at the cut stem projecting out. Using a light turn, tie in the feather flatly, concave side up (curve up), over the pheasant-fiber section; both the pheasant section and hen saddle should be tied in at the same place. Add a few tight, securing thread turns.

## Tying In The Wing Case Fibers And Legs— Problems, Solutions, And Suggestions

1. It is easiest to tie in the hen-saddle section if you expose some of the drawn-back fibers, not just the 1/8 inch of drawn-forward fibers, from your left hand—this gets the hand back a bit, out of the way.

2. The best way to get the hen saddle tied in flatly is to be certain that you hold it flat against the thumb of your left hand to begin with. Then you can simply lower the feather to the hook with your thumb on top and be assured of proper positioning.

3. As we've seen before, torque is always at work—tying in the pheasant fibers and hen saddle slightly to your side of the hook should make them end up right on top.

## Wrapping And Ribbing
## The Abdomen And Thorax

Snip at a slant the butts of the pheasant fibers and the tied-in tips of the hen saddle. Bind these under the thread as you work it forward to a point 1/8 inch behind the eye. Stroke the hen saddle and all the pheasant fibers lightly forward and bind them under two moderate-tension thread turns. (Don't worry about how this looks; it is simply a method of holding these materials out of your way temporarily.) Wrap the yarn in tight, close turns up to the rear of the bound fibers and hackle. Back off the two thread turns to release the pheasant fibers and the hackle. Draw them both back, and then wrap the yarn forward and tie it off 1/8 inch behind the eye; the yarn should be secured under a few tight thread turns.

Draw the pheasant fibers and hackle forward again, and again bind them out of your way with two thread turns. Spiral the V-rib up the abdomen in six to eight tight turns to the rear of the bound fibers and hackle. Once again, back off the two thread turns and then draw back the fibers and hackle. Cover the thorax in only three well-spaced wraps of the V-rib. Secure the end of the V-rib with several tight thread turns at the same place you secured the end of the yarn. Trim the ends of both the yarn and V-rib closely.

6. Snip a section from a pheasant tail.

7. Advance the thread to just past midshank; tie in the pheasant-tail section.

8. Draw back most of the fibers on the prepared hen hackle and tie it in by the stem and few remaining fibers over the pheasant section.

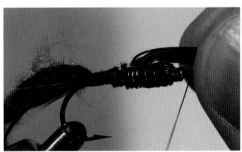

9. Advance the thread, draw the pheasant and hen forward, and secure both with two turns of thread.

10. Wrap the yarn to the pheasant, back off the two thread turns, draw the pheasant and hen back, wrap the yarn up the thorax, tie off the yarn.

**11.** Rib the abdomen and thorax by following the same proceedure you did for the yarn with the V-rib.

**12.** Pull the hackle forward over the thorax, trim it, and secure it with turns of thread.

**13.** Pull the pheasant section forward and secure it over the hen hackle with turns of thread.

**14.** Trim the yarn's and V-rib's ends, cover them with dubbing, build a thread head and complete it as usual.

**15.** Trim the center of the hen-hackle tip to create split tails.

# Wrapping And Ribbing The Abdomen And Thorax—Problems, Solutions, And Suggestions

1. You may have to exaggerate the angle of the V-rib when you first begin wrapping it, as it has a tendency to slip back off the yarn; but as soon as the first half of the first turn is secure you can wrap the V-rib at an appropriate angle.

2. The Morristone has a lot of ribs, but I suggest you resist the temptation to use less—real stoneflies have many abdominal segments, which the ribs suggest (on a larger hook you could increase the number of turns to as many as ten). A stonefly's thorax consists of three segments, hence the three ribs through the thorax.

3. In tying the Rick's Caddis and the Gold Ribbed Hare's Ear, you probably noticed that wrapping materials over the ends of a layer of lead takes some tying adjustments and by now, you probably realize that a double layer of lead requires even more. Winding tension with materials, extra turns of materials or thread at the ends of the lead, and varying the winding angle of body materials and ribs are all ways of tackling the trouble spots at the lead's blunt ends.

# The Legs, Wing Case, And Final Steps

Draw the hen saddle forward flatly onto the top of the thorax. Looking down the fly from its front (if you can't do this comfortably with a bit of neck craning, you may have to stand for a moment), note where the hen-saddle reaches the front of the yarn-and-V-rib thorax; trim the fibers along both sides of the stem from this point forward. With your left hand, work a couple of thread turns over the trimmed stem as you hold the stem under moderate tension with your right hand. Release the stem and add a few tight securing thread turns. Draw the pheasant section firmly forward and down on top of the hackle. Secure the pheasant section in the same manner as you did the saddle hackle. Lift the hackle tip and pheasant-section tip together and trim both closely as one.

Bind the cut ends under thread, and then spin a bit of brown dubbing onto the thread. Cover the bound ends under the dubbing, and then draw back the dubbing with the triangle, or a bit of moisture, as you form a thread head. Secure the head with three half hitches.

Remove the fly from your vise and hold it by its bend. Tease two to four fibers away from each side of the feather tail with your fingers or the closed blades of your scissors. Snip out the center of the feather leaving the two side bunches of fibers. All that remains to complete the Morristone is a bit of head cement on its thread head.

# The Legs, Wing Case, And Final Steps— Problems, Solutions, And Suggestions

1. There is no need to trim the fibers at the tip of the saddle hackle very closely unnecessarily risking a cut stem and ruined fly.

2. Draw the hackle forward over the thorax under no more than *moderate* tension; it can take only this much without breaking.

3. By gripping the pheasant section flatly at its base and then loosening your grip slightly and sliding it down the section once or twice, you can reform the section and restore its flatness for the best possible wing case.

4. Keep the dubbed section in front of the wing case short and full—it is meant to represent the insect's head.

5. By not trimming the center of the hen-saddle tip too closely, you will leave a tiny stub of fibers between the two tails—this helps keep them separate.

# PHEASANT TAIL

As I've mentioned, the Gold Ribbed Hare's Ear is probably the most popular nymph in America and, if that is so, the Pheasant Tail is surely next in line. There is good reason for this: The Pheasant Tail is convincing to trout, relatively easy to tie, and its construction is quite ingenious.

The pattern shown below is, to the best of my knowledge, Al Troth's version of Frank Sawyer's pattern. I have seen the Pheasant Tail in several variations, but this one has emerged (in my experience) as the American standard.

This pattern surprised me at first, as I am sure it has other fly tiers, because pheasant-tail fibers are used to create so many parts of the fly—tail, abdomen, wing case, and legs. Even more surprising is how these fibers suggest each of these parts so effectively. Some tie the Pheasant Tail weighted; I do not. I find that lead really detracts from the tying and appearance of this fly; but of course, you are welcome to try it. Fish the Pheasant Tail as you would the Gold Ribbed Hare's Ear.

## PHEASANT TAIL

**Hook:** Regular wire, regular shank or 1 or 2X long, sizes 20 to 10.
**Thread:** Brown, 8/0 or 6/0.
**Tail:** Pheasant-tail fibers.
**Abdomen:** Pheasant-tail fibers.
**Rib:** Small copper wire.
**Thorax:** Peacock herl.
**Wing Case And Legs:** Pheasant-tail fibers.

## The Tails, Rib, And Abdomen

Begin with a size-12 nymph-style hook (the hook shown is an Eagle Claw model No. D57). Start the thread slightly forward of the shank's center, and then spiral it quickly to the bend. Draw four to six fibers to a right angle to the quill of a pheasant-tail feather. (Sometimes these feathers have identical fibers on both sides, and sometimes there is a bright, well-marked row on one side and a dull, faintly marked row on the other; use the bright, well-marked fibers, as these are the most durable.) Snip the fibers close to the quill, measure them, and then tie them in as a tail at the bend; tail length should equal 1/2 to 2/3 the length of the shank. Lift the butts of the fibers, and spiral the thread back to its starting point at just past midshank; lower the butts and secure them with thread.

Use a light turn to tie in some copper wire. Add several tight securing thread turns, and then trim the butts of the pheasant fibers (and, if necessary, the end of the wire). Lift the wire and wrap the thread down it to the bend. Secure the wire there with thread turns. Snip off five or six

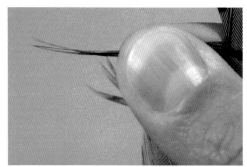

**1.** Draw the fibers of a pheasant tail to a right angle to the quill to square their tips. Snip off the fibers, measure them, tie them in as a tail, and tie in the copper wire.

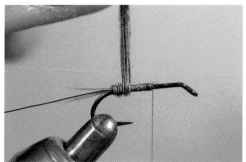
**2.** Tie in more pheasant-tail fibers and wrap them up the abdomen.

**3.** Square, measure, and then tie in the wing-case fibers.

**4.** Tie in and wrap the peacock herl.

**5.** Rib the abdomen and thorax with the copper wire.

more pheasant-tail fibers (the tips needn't be aligned this time) and use the pinch to tie them in at the bend; tie the fibers in by the last 1/4 inch of their tips. Advance the thread again to its starting point. Draw the fibers into a group and wrap them up the shank in close turns to form the abdomen. When they have reached the thread's starting point, secure the fibers under thread wraps. Trim the butts of the fibers.

## The Tail, Rib, And Abdomen— Problems, Solutions, And Suggestions

1. Stroke the tail fibers a time or two to even their tips before snipping them from the quill.

2. If you carefully tie in the copper wire near its end, you will not need to trim the wire.

3. Once the fibers for the abdomen are tied in, you can control their tips by either pushing them down, in a motion similar to the pinch, and then wrapping the thread forward over them, or you can simply snip the tips off.

4. Loosen your grasp momentarily and slip it down the fibers just a bit before wrapping them up the shank; this will even the tension throughout.

5. Pheasant-tail fibers are fragile, adjust tension accordingly when wrapping them.

6. If the butts of the pheasant fibers keep escaping your grasp as you wrap them, use the first finger of your left hand to press them down against the shank each time they reach the top of the hook; this allows you to bring your right hand around for the next turn each time without the risky passing of the fibers from hand to hand. The difficulty stems from the shortness of the fibers.

7. To keep the fibers from spreading as you wrap them, twist the bunch a bit.

## Tying In The Wing Case Fibers And Wrapping The Thorax

Draw its tips even and then snip off yet another bunch of pheasant-tail fibers; this bunch should consist of about a dozen fibers, which would cover about 1/2 inch of the quill. Tie the fibers in at the front of the abdomen with their tips projecting rearwards; the fibers should project from the tie-in point a distance equal to the full length of the hook. Secure the fibers with several tight thread turns. Trim the butts at an angle, and then bind them with thread. Return the thread to the rear of the thorax.

Select two bushy, long-fibered peacock herls (save the shorter-fibered herls for smaller flies), snip them from the main quill, snip off the last 1/2 inch or so at their butts (too much quill or stem here), and then tie them in by their butts. Trim the herl's stubs. Wrap one herl up to the head area and tie it off. Do the same with the remaining herl. Trim the ends of both herls closely.

## Tying In The Wing Case Fibers And Wrapping The Thorax—Problems, Solutions, And Suggestions

1. It is important to measure the wing-case fibers carefully because the length of the legs will be determined by the length of these fibers.

2. Remember: The wing-case fibers should be tied in slightly forward of midshank.

3. If you are having trouble keeping the herls from sliding down the thorax into a bunched mess, it probably means that you didn't cut the butts of the wing-case fibers at an angle, or at least not enough of an angle. This angle creates a gradual taper which is much easier to wrap the herl over than is a blunt edge. The best you can do in this case is to try to build a taper with thread wraps—and then cut the fibers at a long angle in the future.

4. Check to insure that no thread is showing either behind the wing-case fibers or between them and the peacock-herl thorax—-functionally, this means nothing, but it is none too soon to be taking pride in your tying.

5. It is a good idea to leave even a bit more bare shank for the head of this fly than usual.

**6.** Draw the wing-case fibers forward and secure them with thread turns.

## Ribbing, And Forming The Wing Case And Legs

Wrap the copper wire up the abdomen in five to seven evenly spaced spirals; continue to spiral the wire through the thorax in about three spirals. Tie off and secure the wire; trim the wire closely. Draw the wing-case fibers firmly forward over the top of the thorax and secure them. Draw three to five of the fiber tips jutting forward, toward you and then back; secure them with three thread turns. These fibers should now sweep back along the near side of the thorax. Repeat this process on the far side of the thorax. Trim away the fibers still jutting forward, build a thread head, add half hitches, trim the thread, and complete the fly with a coating of head cement.

## Ribbing, And Forming The Wing Case And Legs—Problems, Solutions, And Suggestions

1. It is easiest to rib the abdomen if you lift the wing-case fibers up out of the way for each turn of wire.

2. The closer you trim the copper wire the better; a pair of worn scissors (worn too much for general fly-tying use) can snip the wire closely with their points.

3. Working the leg fibers to the sides is tricky. I find that it helps to crease the fibers by pushing down firmly against their butts with the flats of the scissors; the leg fibers then stay separate from the rest.

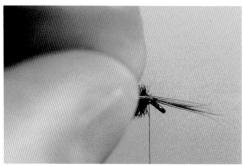

**7.** Draw a few pheasant-tail fibers back along each side of the thorax and bind them with thread.

**8.** Snip closely any remaining fibers and complete the fly.

# SKIP NYMPH DARK

The Skip Nymph Dark is my attempt to borrow the best features from both the Gold Ribbed Hare's Ear and the Pheasant Tail. The simplicity and deadliness of the Gold Ribbed Hare's Ear seems to lie largely in its scruffy hare's mask dubbing, so I took this. The Pheasant Tail offers a copper rib and a pheasant-tail wing case; both of which are somber and natural looking and both of which I also took. It seemed clear that the Gold Ribbed Hare's Ear is too pale to properly match many mayfly nymphs (though it matches some very well); that is why the dyed brown hare's mask was chosen. In the end, and after much experimentation, the tying of the Skip Nymph Dark varies considerably from the tying of either of its models—nevertheless, the inspiration is indeed owed to these two proven nymphs. In honing the tying of the Skip Nymph Dark it proved advantageous to employ only three different materials (hook and thread aside) with each serving more than one function. (The standard Skip Nymph is tied with natural, undyed hare's mask; it is pictured and described in the fly listings in the last section.)

Fish the Skip Nymph as you would the Gold Ribbed Hare's Ear. As with the Gold Ribbed Hare's Ear, you can tie the Skip Nymph either weighted or unweighted.

## SKIP NYMPH DARK

**Hook:** Any regular-shank, 1X or 2X long, heavy wire
nymph hook sizes 20 to 8.
**Thread:** Black or brown 8/0 or 6/0.
**Ribbing:** Small copper wire.
**Abdomen And Thorax:** Fur from a dyed brown
hare's mask (overall, a dark shade).
**Tails And Wing Case:** Pheasant-tail fibers, dark side
up.
**Weight:** Copper or lead wire.

## The Copper Wire, Abdomen, And Tails

Mount a suitable size-10 or size-12 nymph hook (your first tying decision thus far), with its barb smashed, into your vise (the hook shown is a Partridge Captain Hamilton model No. H1A, size 12). Start the thread in the center of the shank. Using a light turn, tie in the copper wire; if you choose to cut the copper wire now, as opposed to leaving it uncut and setting the spool to the left of your vise (see "The Gold Ribbed Hare's Ear"), leave the wire a couple of inches longer than needed.

Hold the wire back along the shank and slightly above it under light tension as you spiral the thread back along it to the bend; when you reach the bend, add several tight securing thread turns. If you tied in the wire near its end you need not trim the remaining stub, but if more than about 1/16 inch of wire projects from the tie-in point, trim it closely. Dub a tapered abdomen from the bend to slightly past the center of the shank.

Draw a 1/2 inch section of pheasant-tail fibers to a right angle to the stem squaring their points, and then cut the section off close to the stem. Measure the section against the hook; then tie it in at the front of the abdomen—the points should project beyond the bend a distance of about 1/2 to 2/3 the shank length and the butts should project forward. The dark side of the fibers should be up and showing.

1. Tie in the copper wire and dub the abdomen. Square the tips of a section of pheasant-tail fibers and tie them in.

Take one turn forward of the copper wire, just enough to start it into the dubbing; hold the wire stationary with your right hand; the wire should project toward you from beneath the hook. Now grasp the tips of the pheasant-tail fibers with your left hand and draw the fibers down along the abdomen. Take one turn of wire over the pheasant-tail section to lock the section in right on top of the abdomen. Maintain constant tension on the wire as you release the tips of the pheasant fibers. Begin spiraling the wire up the abdomen in five to eight turns to the front of the abdomen. Secure the end of the copper wire under several tight thread turns. Do not cut the end of the wire or the butts of the pheasant-tail section.

## The Copper Wire, Abdomen, And Tails— Problems, Solutions, And Suggestions

1. Copper wire is slippery, so really secure it before you begin spiraling the thread down it to the bend.

2. You can allow for the torque of the thread by simply tying in the fibers slightly toward the near side of the hook, and then securing the fibers under the copper wire toward the near side as well—the wire's force will roll the fibers right up on top.

3. Maintaining the original flatness of the pheasant-fiber section is tricky because of the squaring proceedure, but this flatness does produce a more pleasing appearance than do bunched fibers. To regain this flatness, draw the squared tips of the fibers together and hold them as you cut the fibers from the stem; continue holding the fiber tips as you stroke the butts along the flat of the bunch; the fibers should return to their original, flat configuration but now their tips are squared. Bunched or flat: the fish won't care.

## Weighting, Thorax, And Wing Case

Pull the butts of the pheasant fibers back and wrap the thread back over them; the result should be that these fibers will be doubled over for about 1/16 inch and will project back over the abdomen. Wrap the copper wire you left untrimmed (at least it *should* be untrimmed) toward the eye in close turns (as usual, leave room for the thread head); then wrap another layer of wire back to the doubled pheasant fibers and then another layer forward to just short of the end of the first layer—you now have three layers of copper wire to give your fly weight. Trim the end of the copper wire closely and then bind the wire under thread.

Dub the thorax heavily, draw forward and then secure the pheasant-fiber wing case, create a thread head secured with half hitches, cement the head, and then tease out some fur and guard hairs from the sides of the thorax—all just as you did for the Gold Ribbed Hare's Ear. To complete the Skip Nymph Dark, tug two or three fibers out from one, and then the other side of the tail, and then snip the remaining center fibers.

## Weighting Thorax, And Wing Case— Problems, Solutions, And Suggestions

1. In case you are tempted to fold back the end of the copper wire when you fold back the pheasant fibers—don't. The wire should keep projecting forward throughout this step; this will put the end of the wire right in front of the folded, thread-bound fibers just as it should be in preparation for the layering of the wire.

2. As with the Gold Ribbed Hare's Ear, the Skip Nymph can be tied and fished unweighted. The three layers of copper wire offer easily applied, modest weight (in the smaller sizes, the wire actually adds considerable weight), but if you want more weight than this, you would probably do best to substitute one layer of lead.

3. Add the copper wire tapering down to the shank in front (as much as possible) and back against the end of the folded pheasant fibers, but not over them, for the neatest dubbed thorax executed with ease.

**2.** Start the copper wire into the dubbing, draw the pheasant-fiber tips down onto the abdomen, and take a turn of the wire to lock the pheasant-tail fibers in place. Wrap the copper wire up the fibers and dubbing to the end of the abdomen in several ribs. Secure the wire under tight thread turns.

**3.** Draw back the butts of the pheasant-tail fibers and secure them with tight thread turns.

**4.** Add weight by building up three layers of copper wire at the thorax area.

**5.** Dub a thick thorax and then pull the pheasant-tail butts down and secure them over the thorax with thread turns. Complete a thread head and apply head cement to it as usual.

**6.** Snip the center fibers from the tail leaving two separate fiber groups.

# Part-III

# THE BUCKTAIL, STREAMER, AND SOFT HACKLE

## COMPONENTS OF A STREAMER (OR BUCKTAIL)

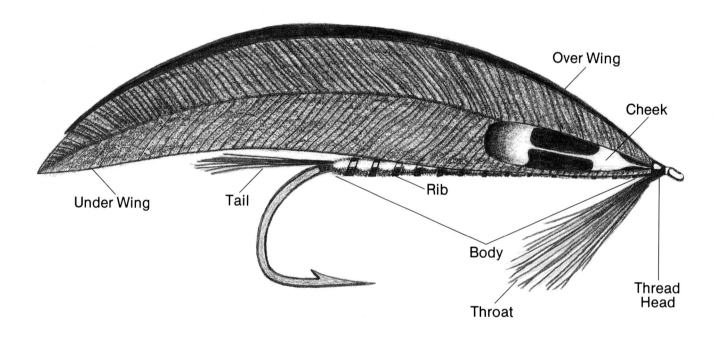

Over Wing

Cheek

Under Wing

Tail

Rib

Body

Throat

Thread Head

Illustration by Tony Amato

Here are some big flies (and a small one) that will teach you to work with a tinsel body, handle floss, create sweeping wings of hair and of feathers, to add hackle to a small fly, and to tie a new finishing knot on your fly heads.

There is a catch-all quality to this section but, as with the last section, I still feel that having a fly order which best serves your progress is more important than having one that makes for slick organization. Actually, the bucktail and streamer make perfect sense together—both are swum to imitate bait fish and the like. The soft hackle doesn't quite fit—it is swum, yes, but not always, and it imitates not a bait fish but an insect. The soft hackle is here because it picks up on the floss-body technique of the previous fly and leads into the hackling technique of the next. Actually, the soft hackle should probably be in the last section and the Woolly Bugger should be in this one. But again: so what? They are in their best places for your tying and learning.

# MICKEY FINN

This time-tested, proven fly was made popular by an angling legend of long ago: John Alden Knight. You will still find the Mickey Finn in the trays of most fly shops—the acid test of any fly's success and popularity.

With the Mickey Finn, you will deal with hand stacking and then creating the hair wing of a "bucktail," a hair-wing fly that imitates a bait fish or some other kind of swimming creature. In the case of the Mickey Finn, it would be hard to say just what that creature might be; but many a trout has confidently clamped its jaws around a

Mickey Finn, so the question is of little consequence. I trust you will not be surprised to find that a bucktail's wing is usually composed of hair from a buck's tail; what *is* surprising is that the part of a fly that makes it look like a fish is called a "wing."

Swim the Mickey Finn slowly or quickly, gracefully or erratically, deep or shallow in streams or lakes for almost any game fish—trout, bass, panfish, and even some saltwater species.

## MICKEY FINN

**Hook:** Any 4X to 6X long hook with medium to heavy wire (some manufacturers will simply call this their "streamer," "bucktail," or "streamer-bucktail" hook) sizes 2 to 12.

**Thread:** Black, 6/0 or 8/0 (although I recommend you begin with 3/0).

**Rib:** Oval silver tinsel.

**Body:** Flat silver tinsel.

**Wing:** Yellow bucktail topped by red bucktail topped by yellow bucktail; the top bunch of yellow bucktail should equal the bulk of the red and lower yellow combined.

## The Tinsel Body

Smash the barb on a size-8 4X long streamer-bucktail hook (the hook shown is a Dai-Riki model 700), and mount it in your vise. Start the thread 1/8 inch behind the eye (again, I suggest you use 3/0 now and switch to a finer thread later when you are more comfortable with the bucktail wing). Using a light turn, tie in the oval silver tinsel. For this hook size I prefer a fine-diameter tinsel. Hold the tinsel at an angle above the shank as you spiral the thread to the bend. Add a few tight securing thread turns there, and then spiral the thread back to its starting point. Snip closely the end of the oval tinsel.

Snip off about 9 inches of medium flat silver tinsel (or leave it attached to the spool until you wrap it). Using a light turn, tie in the flat silver tinsel so that it angles with its stub end forward on the hook's near side with the bulk of the tinsel to the rear of the tie-in point and on the hook's far side. (Mylar tinsel, which is now in common use over the metal tinsels, usually has a gold side and a silver side—tie the silver side up.) Pass the tinsel from hand to hand as you wrap it tightly in consecutive turns to the bend. Upon reaching the bend, wrap the tinsel forward in the

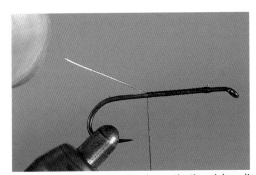

**1.** Tie in the oval silver tinsel and wrap the thread down it to the bend. Add securing thread turns; then spiral the thread forward.

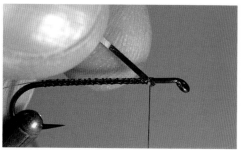

**2.** Tie in the flat silver tinsel.

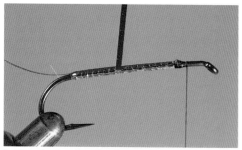

**3.** Wrap the flat silver tinsel to the bend and then forward.

**4.** Rib the flat-tinsel body with the oval silver tinsel.

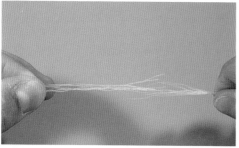

**5.** Snip a bunch of yellow bucktail and pull the short fibers from its base.

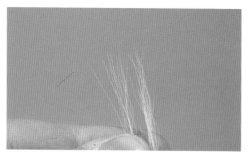

**6.** Grasp the bunch by its tips, draw out the shorter fibers, combine both bunches with tips even.

same manner until you reach the thread's starting point. Tie off the tinsel, add several tight securing thread turns, and trim the end of the tinsel closely.

Spiral the oval silver tinsel tightly up the tinsel body to the thread end in eight to twelve turns. Tie off the oval tinsel at the thread's starting point, trim the oval tinsel's end, and then add several tight securing thread turns. It is advantageous to avoid tying off the oval on top of the fly as this creates a lump which may kick the wing out of position; if this occurs, simply back off the rib and alter the spacing. Wind the thread forward to 1/16 inch behind the eye and then back again to the front of the body—this layer of thread will provide a foundation for the wing.

## The Tinsel Body— Problems, Solutions, And Suggestions

1. Each wrap of flat tinsel should either overlap slightly, or at least touch, the previous wrap. You will find that if you work the tinsel from side to side a bit as you wrap it, it will tend to drop into place. Wrapping the tinsel at an angle that pushes each wrap up against the previous one also helps.

2. If the end of the flat tinsel keeps slipping from your grasp as you wrap, try clamping your hackle pliers onto its end.

## The Bucktail Wing

Bucktail requires some stacking, but the natural-white fibers that dye brightly, the ones you will use here, behave poorly in a hair stacker; therefore, you will hand stack them. Snip some yellow hair from a bucktail. Grasp the hair firmly by the last 1 1/2 inch of its tips. Grasp the hair butts modestly right where they are first exposed with your remaining hand. Draw your hands apart and as you do, the short fibers will come free of the main bunch.

All that remains is to stack (even the tips) of the bunch. Grasp the bunch firmly by its tips, and then draw out the shorter fibers as before. Now you have two bunches. Combine the two bunches so that their tips are even. Repeat this sequence once or twice more until you have a bunch of hairs in which the tips are fairly squared, although they needn't be perfectly squared. Sometimes a few fibers will stubbornly project beyond the squared ends of the bunch despite all your careful stacking; simply draw these out by their tips.

Measure the hair bunch against the hook and note the point where the bunch is about one and a half times as long as the shank. Using the pinch, tie in the hair bunch at this point (remember, the end of the thread should be at the front of the body). Tighten the pinch turn only modestly, and then work the thread forward in a few more turns, each tighter than the one before it. Now continue working the thread forward in tight turns until the thread's end is halfway between the body and the rear of the eye. Lift the butts of the hair with your left hand and trim them closely at an angle. Cover the cut hair butts with thread. Work the thread back to the front of the body and, as with tails, no thread wraps should go farther back than these wraps.

Work the thread to the rear of the head area. Hand stack another bunch of bucktail hair—red this time—and tie it in, trim it, and bind the cut hair ends with thread, all just as you did the first bunch.

With the thread again at the rear of the head area, stack, tie in, trim, and bind the cut ends of another yellow bunch of bucktail; this bunch, however, should be equal in bulk to the first two bunches combined. If all the hair butts are bound under thread, all that remains is to tie off the thread and add head cement, but you will tie off the thread this time with the fly tier's standard finishing knot: the whip finish.

# The Bucktail Wing—
# Problems, Solutions, And Suggestions

1. Too much hair is awkward to work with and unnecessary; study the photographs to determine the proper amount. If your hair wing seems unweildy, experiment.

2. Bucktail is stiff, slippery stuff; secure it well, or it will slip when you trim its butts. Raising and trimming the butts carefully and gently also helps.

3. Remember, the first thread turns on each hair bunch are light, but be certain you have at least a few turns that are really tight before you trim the hair butts.

4. Trim the hair butts with care, at the angle pictured, and you will be assured of a neat thread head.

5. If your Mickey Finn's wing seems to lower over and hide the body, try tying in the first hair bunch slightly forward of the body, just three or four close thread turn's forward, taking a moderate-tension thread turn around the hair *only*, and then wrapping back over the hair to the front of the body. The single turn around the hair will really prop it up.

6. Wrapping thread over a steep taper, as you have at the trimmed ends of the bucktail, can be tricky; the thread tends to slide down the taper in a tangle. Here is how I avoid the problem: At the front of the head area, right behind the eye, I make my thread turns as tight as possible, a sort of anchor, and then work the thread up the taper in progressively lighter turns. These lighter-tension turns are still tight, but not quite so tight as the anchor turns. At the rear half of the head there is little taper, so thread turns here can be very tight. Working the thread forward, down the taper, lighten the thread's tension again.

7. You can spread the taper of the head by trimming the butts of each hair bunch slightly farther back than the butts of the bunch before it—in other words, each time you trim, trim slightly farther back than the last time.

8. Sometimes it helps to angle the thread turns when binding the hair butts. To do this, tip the top of each turn noticeably farther forward than the bottom.

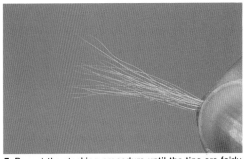

**7.** Repeat the stacking procedure until the tips are fairly even.

**8.** Measure the bunch against the hook.

**9.** Tie in the bunch using the pinch.

**10.** Once the bunch is secured under thread turns, lift and snip its butts.

**11.** The butts should be cut closely, at an angle.

**12.** Bind the butts under thread turns.

**13.** Stack, measure, tie in, trim; then bind the butts of a stack of red bucktail.

**14.** Add final bunch of yellow bucktail; this bunch should equal the bulk of the first two combined.

**15.** Start the whip finish as you would a half hitch; slip the loop over the thread head.

**16.** Lift up firmly on the working side of the loop and release the passive side.

**17.** Pass the working side from hand to hand as you add three turns over the passive side.

**18.** Close the loop as usual.

# The Whip Finish

The whip finish has intimidated more than one fly tier, which is a shame, because the whip finish is really only a half hitch that forgot to stop—it's easy. Look at it this way, the half hitch is a loop in which one of its sides is wrapped around the other; the whip finish is created when the side of the loop doing the wrapping adds more than one wrap.

Begin by adding a half hitch at the rear of the thread-head, but stop as soon as the half-hitch loop is hooked over the head. At this point, you have the side of the loop that is doing the wrapping, which we will call the "working" side, and the side of the loop which is being wrapped over, which we will call the "passive" side. The working side should be nearest you, and the passive side will be farthest from you. Grasp the working side in your left hand and hold it straight up under tension; then remove your right-hand fingers from the loop. As long as tension is maintained on the working side, it should keep the passive side firmly locked in place.

Now all you need to do is maintain tension on the working side as you pass it from hand to hand and wrap it towards the eye in three turns; as you do this, keep the passive side out in front of the fly—don't let the passive side slip behind the working side, or the turns you are adding will fail to enhance the whip finish's security. Close the whip-finish loop as you would a half-hitch loop, trim the thread, and add head cement.

# The Whip Finish—
# Problems, Solutions, And Suggestions

1. Forming an extra-large loop can make the whip finish easier to execute.

2. Never release tension on the working side once it has locked the passive side in place; to do so will let the bobbin drop and the loop snap closed.

3. Again, you must keep the passive side forward, off the eye, throughout the execution of the whip finish. Just tug it out that way now and then, or hold it there with whichever hand is free.

4. Waxing the thread can help; it makes the passive side stiff enough to stay forward on its own.

## THE WHIP FINISH

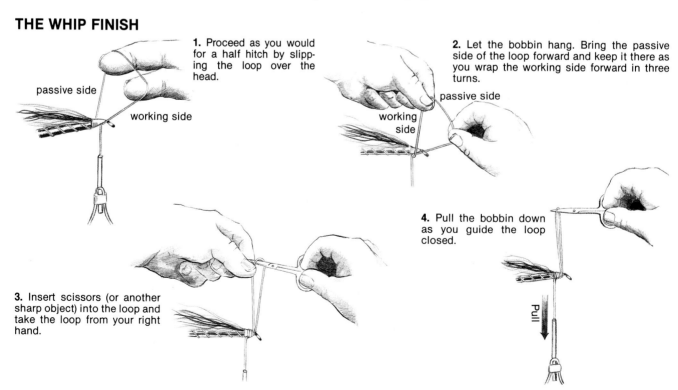

passive side

working side

**1.** Proceed as you would for a half hitch by slipping the loop over the head.

**2.** Let the bobbin hang. Bring the passive side of the loop forward and keep it there as you wrap the working side forward in three turns.

passive side

working side

**3.** Insert scissors (or another sharp object) into the loop and take the loop from your right hand.

**4.** Pull the bobbin down as you guide the loop closed.

Pull

# BLACK GHOST

Because it has long hackle-wings swept back over its body and is tied on a long-shank hook and swum beneath the surface, the Black Ghost is a streamer; and it is a classic. Here, you will learn to create a floss body, a beard hackle, and streamer wings.

## BLACK GHOST

**Hook:** Any 4X to 6X long hook with medium to heavy wire (some manufacturers will simply call this a "streamer," "bucktail," or "streamer-bucktail" hook) sizes 4 to 12.
**Thread:** Black 8/0 or 6/0.
**TAIL:** Yellow hackle fibers.
**Rib:** Medium-fine flat silver tinsel.
**Body:** Black floss.
**Throat:** Yellow hackle fibers.
**Wing:** Four white hackles.
**Cheek:** (optional) jungle cock eyes or substitute.

## The Tail, Body, And Rib

Begin by smashing the barb on a size-4, 4X to 6X long streamer-bucktail hook (the hook pictured is a Gamakatsu model Fly 16) and mount it in your vise. Start the thread about 1/16 inch behind the eye and spiral it to the bend. Draw to a right angle to the stem a section of yellow hackle fibers and then strip them free. Measure the fibers against the hook, and tie them in using the pinch; the length of the tail should equal the hook's *gape* (note: in the past we have always measured materials against the shank, but not this time). Add a few securing thread turns; then lift the butts of the fibers, spiral the thread forward, lower the butts and tie them in using the pinch. Advance the thread to its starting point.

Using a light turn, tie in some medium-fine flat silver tinsel. If you are using two-color mylar tinsel, tie it in gold side up. (This is in contrast to the silver-side-up approach we used on the Mickey Finn; this is a different technique.) Add a few securing thread turns, and then lift the tinsel and spiral the thread down it to the bend. Trim the tinsel's stub end if necessary

Return the thread to its starting point again and tie in some black floss. I always buy the single-strand floss rather than the four-strand— single strand is easiest to control, least likely to become tangled on the spool, and I always have the option of doubling it over once or twice should I need it thicker. For now I suggest you use single strand for the Black Ghost's body. Tie in the floss at the thread's starting point using the

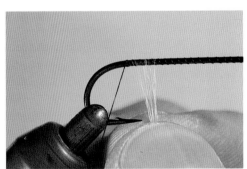

1. Measure the tail fibers and tie them in at the bend.

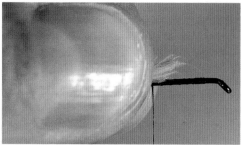

**2.** Advance the thread; then tie in the butts of the fibers using the pinch.

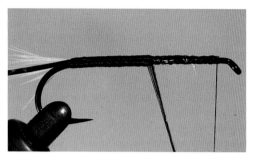

**3.** Tie in the tinsel, tie in the floss, and wrap a floss body.

**4.** Lift and fold the tinsel.

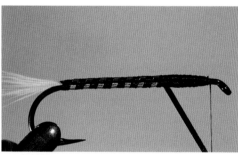

**5.** Spiral the tinsel up the floss body.

**6.** Strip another bunch of hackle fibers, invert the hook, and use the pinch to tie in the fibers as a beard.

pinch, add several tight securing tread turns, lift the floss and spiral the thread down it to the bend, and then trim the stub end of the floss. Spiral the thread back to its starting point.

Wrap the floss in close turns up the shank, and tie it off at the thread's starting point; trim its end closely. Lift the tinsel and *fold* it where it projects from the bend so that the silver side is up. Wrap the tinsel up the floss body in seven to ten evenly spaced ribs, secure the end of the tinsel with a few tight thread wraps, and snip the tinsel's stub end.

## The Tail, Body, And Rib— Problems, Solutions, And Suggestions

1. If you prefer the tail gathered a bit, tie it in just short of the bend, and then lift it and wrap the thread down it in turns of only moderate tension. From here, proceed as before.

2. Floss is easily frayed; try to avoid sliding your fingers across it. If your fingertips are rough, apply a skin lotion to them or sand them lightly with fine sandpaper (400 grit or finer).

3. Floss tends to spread which often helps it go on smoothly, but if it spreads too much, twist it a bit.

4. Unless you have some very long hackle fibers for the tail, there will be a thin spot ahead of the end of the tail fibers resulting in a floss body thin in front and thicker at the rear. You can compensate for this by wrapping the floss to the thread's starting point, wrapping it back again to the end of the tail's butts, and then wrapping it forward again; now the body will be fuller in the front than the rear.

5. The ribs should never be closer together than the tinsel's width and should usually be a bit wider.

## The Beard Hackle

Remove the hook from your vise. Invert it and return it to your vise. Draw to a right angle to the stem a section of yellow hackle fibers and then strip them free. Measure, and then tie in the fibers at the front of the body using the pinch; the fibers should project from their tie-in point the same distance as the tails do from theirs. Add a few tight securing thread turns. Lift and trim the butts closely.

## The Beard Hackle— Problems, Solutions, And Suggestions

1. If the fibers tend to roll around the hook, hold them tightly as you add the tight securing thread turns; you can even pull the fibers slightly toward you to counter the thread's torque.

2. The beard hackle can be tied in without inverting the hook for expediency, but for now I recommend inverting.

## The Streamer Wing And The Jungle Cock Eye

Almost any hackle can be used for streamer wings—large dry-fly hackle, dry-fly saddle hackle, and even hen-cape hackle—but the best streamer hackles are long, fairly wide, and somewhat webby. One of the best sources I have found for streamer wings is the cheaper domestic rooster necks. Although these come from the same section of a rooster as do dry-fly hackles, the necks I speak of are bred for different qualities—exactly the qualities desirable in streamer wings. Nobody seems certain as to just what these necks should be called, but if you ask for a rooster neck with streamer hackles on it, that should make it clear enough. If you don't have ideal streamer hackles, use whatever you have—the fish will surely meet you halfway.

Wrap a layer of thread to just behind the eye, and then back to the front of the body. Select and pluck two appropriate-size hackles from each side of a cape (study the photographs to help you determine the appropriate size). If you are using loose hackle, as saddles sometimes are, select two sets of feathers similar in size and form; try to match the hackle sets so they will cup together well and once cupped, both sets will have straight stems or stems that curve down at their tips when viewed along their flats—the point is that you want the feathers to match and to curve down, or not at all, instead of up.

Measure one of the hackles along the hook. At the point where it is one and a half times the shank's length, strip its stem beyond this. Use this hackle as a guide to strip the other hackles, and then return them to their original sets. Cup the hackle sets together, stripped stems all starting at the same place. Grasp the hackle's stems between your thumb and finger, your finger below and your thumb on top; the hackle's flats should be vertical (see photograph). This aligns the stems. Pinch the hackles together from their sides, just back from the stripped stems. Hold the hackles, flats vertical, stems parallel with the shank, to the top of the hook; the stems, just ahead of where their fibers start, should touch the front of the body on top of the hook. No need for the pinch here; instead, make three moderate-tension thread turns over the stems. Follow this with three tighter turns, and finally three really tight turns. Release the hackles and see if they sit in two neatly cupped sets directly over the shank. If you are not satisfied with their position, unwrap the thread holding them and try it again. Carefully lift the stems and trim them closely.

You can certainly skip the jungle cock eyes—they are expensive, sometimes difficult to obtain, and of questionable value from a fishing perspective—but if you are going to add them, now is the time. Strip any fuzzy fibers from the stem and sides of the feather leaving a clean eye. Hold one feather parallel with the shank and sweeping back along the body and secure it by its stem at the thread head. Do the same on the far side of the fly. Trim the jungle cock's stems.

Whether or not you added the cheeks of jungle cock, build a thread head, add a triple whip finish (a three-turn whip finish), trim the thread, and add head cement.

## The Streamer Wing And The Jungle Cock Eye Problems, Solutions, And Suggestions

1. By all means, don't skip the double layer of thread that forms a foundation for the head—it really helps lock the wing in.

2. To keep the two feather-groups separate, use the measuring hackle to measure, and then strip the other hackle of its group. Set the newly stripped hackle aside. When you measure and strip the two hackles from the other group, strip each on one side only; then regroup both sets. Once the hackles are back in their original sets, finish stripping the second set. As long as the hackles of one set are only half stripped, there can be no doubt as to which hackles belong together.

3. To help the hackle-wing lay down, you can strip the bottoms of the hackles slightly farther than at their tops, in this case about 1/16 to 1/8 inch at most. This can be done when the hackles are first stripped, or you can strip the extra when the wing is aligned in your left hand and ready to mount.

4. You can also trim the wing-stems *before* you mount the wings; this eliminates the problem of the wings shifting when you lift their stems to trim them. Just be sure that if you do trim the stems first, that you don't

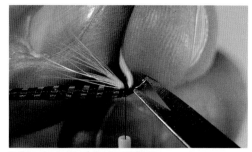

7. Trim the butts of the beard fibers.

8. Select two matching sets of hackles for wings.

9. Measure and prepare the wing hackles.

10. Hold all four hackles by the stems to align them.

11. Tie in the wing using progressively tighter turns of thread.

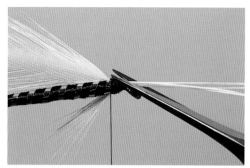

**12.** Snip the hackle stems.

**13.** Jungle cock is optional; shown is a prepared eye on the left and one unprepared on the right.

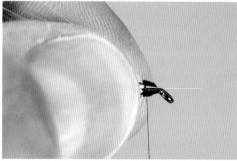

**14.** Tie in an eye on each side.

**15.** Snip the eye's stems and complete the fly.

trim too short; but if you do, simply strip off a few more hackle fibers.

5. To quote A. K. Best from his book *Production Fly Tying:* "If you're having trouble with one or more of your feathers wanting to twist or roll on its side, you can do one or both of the following: 1. Reverse the order of the feathers; that is, place the inside feather on the outside. 2. Flatten the butts slightly with a needle-nose pliers. If you absolutely cannot get the feather to flatten where you want it, select another neck and start over. Some necks contain feathers whose quill stems will not do anything you want. Don't fight it — the quill stems always win." A.K. ties more flies in half a year than most anglers will tie in a lifetime — could there be a source of advice more sound?

6. There are some good substitutes for expensive, often hard-to-obtain jungle cock. Synthetic jungle cock is one. You can also snip a jungle-cock shape out of a guinea feather — simply find a dot on the stem (guinea feathers have dots everywhere) and snip around it. This idea I got from fly tier-author Dick Talleur.

Frank Amato Photo

# PARTRIDGE AND YELLOW SOFT HACKLE

Sylvester Nemes rediscovered an unusual fly and developed some unusual methods for fishing it. In 1975 he revealed these efforts to the fly-fishing world in his book *The Soft Hackled Fly*. What he rediscovered is a simple, bare-bones fly that looks exactly like nothing but suggests a lot, and what it usually suggests are hatching mayflies, caddisflies, and even stoneflies. "Soft hackles," as these flies are often called, may be fished in a variety of manners: just under the surface dead drift, twitched or swum (or, as fly fishing author Dave Hughes described it to me, "coaxed") across the current, or even floated dead drift to imitate a spent, bedraggled caddisfly (an approach from fly-fishing artist Richard Bunse).

The Partridge and Yellow Soft Hackle we will explore here is only one of many variations—other body colors and materials, other hackle colors and types, and even variations of hook styles (light wire, heavy wire, various shank lengths) are used.

## PARTRIDGE AND YELLOW SOFT HACKLE

**Hook:** Dry fly, standard length, sizes 10 to 16.
**Thread:** Yellow (or simply a pale color), size 8/0 or 6/0.
**Abdomen:** Yellow single-strand floss.
**Thorax:** Hare's mask fur (a thorax is optional).
**Hackle:** Brown hen saddle hackle or partridge flank.

## The Abdomen And Thorax

Smash the barb on a size-12 dry-fly hook (the hook shown is a Daiichi model 1180), and mount it in your vise. Start the thread about 1/16 inch behind the eye, and then use the pinch to tie in the floss. Secure the floss and trim its end. Lift the long end of the floss and spiral the thread down it to the bend; secure the floss at the bend. Spiral the thread forward and stop when it is about two thirds up the shank. Wrap the floss, in close turns, up to the thread and secure its end with the thread; trim the end of the floss. Add hare's ear dubbing to the thread and then dub a short, thick thorax.

**1.** Tie in and wrap a floss body.

## The Abdomen And Thorax— Problems, Solutions, And Suggestions

1. For a thicker abdomen, wrap the floss forward, then rearward, then forward again creating three layers; if you stop the second layer short of the bend, it will give the abdomen a tapered appearance.

2. If you have a floss bobbin, here is a quick way to build the abdomen: Start with the floss, just as you would the thread, by locking the floss over itself and cutting its end; then build the body, work the floss to the thorax area, start the thread *over* the end of the floss, trim the floss's and thread's end together, and continue tying as usual.

**2.** Dub a short, thick thorax.

**3.** Select, measure, and prepare a hen saddle hackle.

**4.** Tie in the hackle as shown, using a light turn.

**5.** Wrap one turn of hackle.

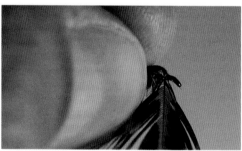

**6.** Draw back the fibers from the first turn of hackle; then add a second turn; repeat this sequence for the third and final turn.

**7.** Tie off the hackle, trim its tip, and complete the fly.

# Hackling

There are a number of ways to hackle this fly; I think it best to start with the easiest. Other methods will be covered in the "Problems, Solutions, and Suggestions" section. In his book *American Nymph Fly Tying Manual*, Randall Kaufmann says:

> Hen saddle feathers are similar to partridge body feathers, but partridge is smaller, less dense, and more difficult for beginning tiers to handle, but it creates an excellent effect.

Hen saddle really is the best choice for your first soft hackle. Switch to partridge later if you like, or just stick with the hen.

I think it also noteworthy that there seems to be considerable disagreement concerning hackle-fiber length for soft-hackles—some experienced tiers prefer that the fibers reach only to the rear of the body; others like the fibers long. The instructions that follow will create a long-fibered soft hackle, but remember that you have options.

Select a brown hen saddle hackle with well-marked, unbroken fibers. Draw the fibers out to a right angle on one side, either side, of the stem. Measure the fibers against the hook; note the place where the hackle has fibers of a length equal to the distance from behind the eye to the rear extremity of the hook, and then strip the fibers from this point to the base of the stem—on both sides. If you prefer, you can use a hackle gauge—simply look for the fibers of appropriate length for a hook two sizes larger than the one you are using (this means that for your size 12 hook, you want a size 8 hackle).

Tie in the hackle at the front of the thorax using a light turn followed by a few tight securing thread turns. Try to tie in the hackle so that its tip projects from the far side of the hook slanting back, the hackle lays on its side with its fibers pointing up and down from the stem, and its cupped face is to the back. Trim the hackle's stem. Get a good grip with your hackle pliers; their jaws should be well into the hackle's tip. This hackle is somewhat fragile, so use light pressure as you wrap it in one turn. With your left hand, draw back all the hackle fibers from this first turn using a sort of loose triangle; then take another turn of hackle. Draw this one back with the triangle as before and add the third and final turn of hackle. Now you should have three close, consecutive turns of hackle.

Secure the hackle's tip with two or three thread turns, trim, draw back the hackle fibers with the triangle as you build a thread head, trim the thread, and add head cement to complete the Partridge and Yellow (Hen and Yellow?) Soft Hackle.

# Hackling— Problems, Solutions, And Suggestions

1. Many tiers prefer to draw the fibers back from the tip of the hackle (hen or partridge body), tie the hackle in by its tip, and then wrap the hackle by holding its butt. The tricky part is judging the fiber length—starting too near the tip will require too many hackle turns to reach the fibers of appropriate length, but starting too far down the hackle will put the appropriate fibers onto the hook too soon. Despite this, once you get used to just how long the fibers need to be, this tip-first method will come quickly and easily. (See "Tying in the Wingcase Fibers and Legs" in "The Morristone.")

2. Some of the keener anglers I know (Dave Hughes, Rick Hafele and Richard Bunse in particular) are tying their soft hackles with sparser hackles than before—let's face it, real caddisflies and mayflies have only six legs. The best way to accomplish this is to strip one side of the hen or partridge, and then wind the stripped feather in only two or three turns.

# Part-IV

# DRY FLIES

## COMPONENTS OF A DRY FLY

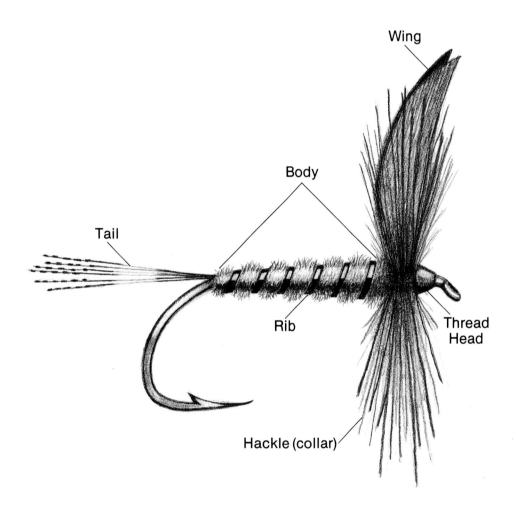

Illustration by Tony Amato

As a rule dry flies are easier to fish but harder to tie than nymphs—that rule, however, is made hazy by a fog of exceptions. Still, of the flies in this book, dry flies *are* the most difficult to tie. But "difficult" is a relative term, and your tying experience at this point will make this next section a challenge you can handle comfortably.

What makes a dry fly a dry fly is that it floats. The final fly in this book is sort of a dry fly; "sort of" because it sort of floats and sort of doesn't—it is the Griffith's Gnat, and it is fished awash, half submerged, to suggest an insect struggling to emerge through the water's surface.

In this section you will learn some traditional flies and some proven, popular newcomers that are unorthodox both in their tying and concept. You will also wet your feet in the tying of tiny flies—for today's tier and fly fisher, an absolute requirement.

# THE ADAMS
## And The
## Classic Dry Fly

I didn't choose the Adams to impress anyone with my originality—nearly every fly-tying book includes it in one form or another. I chose it because it is a good example of the classic dry fly, has proven itself an effective imitation of many insects, and may well be the most popular dry fly in America. The Adams falls neatly into the category of classic dry flies; some of which are also referred to as "Catskill" dry flies because they were developed on the streams of the Catskill Mountains of the East. But the Adams was actually christened on the Boardman River in Michigan and created by Len Halliday.

Learning to tie the Adams is, for all practical purposes, learning to tie a lot of dry flies—the same procedures, steps, and sequence of steps that create it will create many other dry flies by simply varying colors and materials. As there are a few other wing and body types common to standard dry flies (though the basic tying procedure stays the same), I will cover them in this section also.

The Adams is usually fished dead drift, but some twitch it to suggest an active mayfly or caddis.

## ADAMS

**Hook:** Standard dry fly (light wire, regular shank) sizes 20 to 10.
**Thread:** Black, 8/0 or 6/0.
**Wings:** Grizzly hen-saddle tips.
**Tail:** Grizzly and brown hackle fibers.
**Body:** Dubbed muskrat fur.
**Hackle:** Brown and grizzly.

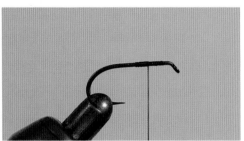

1. Start the thread, wrap it back just short of the shank's center; then wrap it forward just short of the center of this first wrap.

2. Size and select two dry-fly hackles; then set them aside. Pluck two hackles from a grizzly hen saddle neck for wings.

## Tying In The Wings

Using a hackle gauge, or by measuring against the gape, select one size-12 grizzly dry-fly hackle and one brown one. Strip the soft base fibers from the stems (for more information on hackles and hackle preparation refer back to "The Woolly Bugger"). If you are measuring against the gape, the rule is that the fibers should be one and a half to two times as long as the width of the gape. Personally, I lean towards the one-and-a-half size. When sizing a dry-fly hackle, I prefer to gauge the hackle by its longest usable fibers—in other words, if the longest hard, stiff fibers are one and a half times the hook gape I've found my hackle.

Mount a size 12 dry-fly hook in your vise (the hook shown is a Mustad model 94840). Start the thread 1/16 inch behind the eye, and then wrap a thread layer to just short of the shank's center; wrap the thread forward again to just short of the center of the first layer of thread.

Select two matching, medium-size hackles from a grizzly hen neck and pluck them. Turn the hackles so that they are back to back, tips curving away from one another. Pinch the hackles in your left hand, and adjust them so that their tips are even. Measure the hackles against the hook and note the point where the hackles are exactly equal to the distance from the tip of the eye to the middle of the bend (by the "middle," I mean between the far edge of the bend and the point where it begins).

Put the hackles to the hook so that this point is at the thread end. Use the pinch to tie in the hackle wings; the hackles should be projecting forward and should be right on top of the hook with their flats neatly vertical. Add a few securing thread turns; then wrap the thread down the hackle butts to midshank. Lift the butts, and trim them at an angle.

## Tying In The Wings—
## Problems, Solutions, And Suggestions

1. Dry-fly hackles usually have a length of equal-length fibers that tiers call a "sweet spot." A hackle gauge can help you find the sweet spot; strip all the fibers below it.

2. The first two layers of thread create a foundation for the wings. But they also help determine proportions, so apply them accurately.

3. The best hackle-tip wings I've found come from a hen- hackle *neck*, but tips from large dry-fly rooster neck and saddle hackles are accep-table.

4. Double check the length of your wings by measuring them after they are tied in against the blades of your scissors. You can use the scissors' spread points as you would a protractor, or use the length of the blades and mark the wing length on them with your thumb.

5. With grizzly-hackle wings, you can use the black and white bars to help you mark points for measuring, but remember—most wings are without these bars, so avoid depending a lot on this trick.

6. Once the wings are tied in with the pinch, add no thread wraps over them forward of this point—old rule, but particularly important here.

## The Tail And Body

Bind the butts of the wing hackles with thread, and then bring the thread to about the last quarter of the shank before the bend. Stroke a few fibers, say five or six, to a right angle to the stem of a grizzly dry-fly hackle, and then strip them free; these will be for the tail. The best hackles for tails come from the sides of the neck and are called "spade" hackles; use a large spade hackle. Measure the fibers, and then tie them in about midshank using the pinch; the fibers should extend from the *bend* one full hook's length. Strip and then tie in a bunch of brown hackle fibers over the grizzly ones. Make the bunch of brown fibers about twice as big as the grizzly one, and make sure that the tips of all the fibers are even. Strip another batch of grizzly fibers, the same size as the first, and tie them in over the brown.

Secure all the fibers with thread turns, and then lift the fibers slightly as you wrap the thread down them to the bend. Add a few securing thread turns. Spiral the thread forward to the tail's tie-in point. Snip the tail butts at an angle, and then wrap up them to just past midshank. Spiral the thread back to the bend. Snip some muskrat fur from the hide, and spin it onto your thread. Dub a tapered body to just past midshank.

## The Tail And Body—
## Problems, Solutions, And Suggestions

1. To avoid waste, leave the spade hackles for tail fibers on the neck; this way they are easy to find. When a hackle is used up, pluck and discard it.

2. The tightness of the thread turns at the bend will determine how much the tails flare—tight turns will flare the tail while lighter tension turns will group the fibers. For a fly meant to be fished (as opposed to a display fly), I prefer the flared tail fibers for realism.

**3.** Hold the hen hackles in your left hand; even the tips.

**4.** Measure the hen hackles against the hook.

**5.** Tie them in using the pinch.

## SPADE HACKLES FOR TAILS

**6.** Tie in three bunches of hackle fibers for tails.

**7.** Lift the hackle fibers as you wrap the thread down them and the shank to the bend.

**8.** Dub the body.

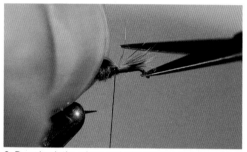

**9.** Draw back the wings and trim the fibers at their base, then add a few thread turns in front to hold them upright.

**10.** Prepare the hackles by stripping the fibers from their bases.

**11.** Tie in and trim the stems of the hackles.

3. You can create a tapered body two ways: Back the dubbing over itself as needed, or add the dubbing to the thread in a tapered manner. Either way works fine.

## Setting The Wings, And Tying In The Hackles

Work the thread up right behind the wing's tie-in point. Pinch the wings along their flats with your left hand, and lift them sharply up, and then back. Apply a bit of pressure as you do this in order to train them to stand up. With your right hand, snip away the fibers in front of the wings near the hook. Add tight thread turns right up against the front of the wings to lock them upright. Release the wings; if they are not vertical, or nearly so, pull them back again, and add more tight thread turns at their base.

Take up the grizzly hackle and the brown hackle you sized earlier. Return the thread to the front of the body (just short of mid shank). Lay the two hackles together with their curves matching, one hackle cupped inside the other; the first fibers beyond the bare stems should start at the same point for both hackles. Set the hackles to the hook at the front of the body with their tips on the far side of the hook and their stripped stems on the near side; the hackles should be on their sides, flat surfaces vertical, and the cupped side of the hackles, the concave side, should face back towards the tail. Tie in both hackles using a light turn followed by a few securing thread turns.

Wrap the thread forward over the two hackle stems nearly to the wings; then stop. Lift and snip the hackle stems closely and at a slight angle. Make sure the stems are trimmed short of the wings, because the stout stem ends could push the wings out of position. Advance the thread to 1/16 inch short of the eye.

## Setting The Wings And Tying In The Hackles Problems, Solutions, And Suggestions

1. The best place to grasp the wings in order to draw them back is at their centers; avoid grasping them by their points for this.

2. To really set the wings upright, hold them back as you set your thumbnail against the front of the grizzly wings and then roll the nail back to kink the stems.

3. Stripping the fuzz from dry-fly hackles can be deceptive—how much is too much; how fuzzy must fibers be to be stripped? One good indicator is hackle length; what you want remaining is a section of fibers similar in length, so bend the hackle and check for this. In most cases I strip no less than 1/3 and often nearly half the length of the stem in order to get to the right fibers.

4. If you leave just a bit of bare stem between the fibers and the tie-in point, say 1/16 inch, the hackles will tend later to perform best.

5. Another way to tie in the hackles, which I have found produces the best results, is to tie in one hackle above the shank (tip on the far side) and one hackle beneath the shank (tip on the near side); both hackles should still curve back.

## Wrapping The Hackles

Clamp the tip of one hackle in your hackle pliers. Begin winding the hackle to the wings; leave a small space between turns, about one stem's width. You should reach the wings in about three or four turns. Try to avoid contact between the wings and the hackle's stem as you wrap the hackle around, and then in front of them. Four or five more spirals should bring the hackle to the thread's end. Tie off the hackle there with three tight thread turns. Release your plier's grip on the hackle, but don't yet trim the hackle's tip.

Grasp the other hackle with your pliers and repeat the process, again trying to avoid pressing the wings out of position with the hackle's stem. Both by feel and by sight, try to wind the second hackle in the space left between the turns of the first hackle. Tie off the tip of the second hackle as you did the first, and again release the pliers.

Lift the two hackle tips together as one and snip them off closely. Also, trim closely any wild hackle fibers that project around the head area. Draw back the hackle fibers with the triangle, form a thread head, add a triple whip finish, trim the thread end, tug the wings slightly apart and add head cement.

That completes the Adams. Later I will show you some alternate wing and body types that will allow you to tie many standard dry flies.

## Wrapping The Hackles— Problems, Solutions, And Suggestions

1. If you can't seem to make the second hackle drop into the slot between the turns of the first, you will still have an effective fly. But it's worth working at this; it will make hackling smooth and neat.

2. Here again, you would be wise to develop your touch—learn to wrap a hackle tightly without breaking it.

3. Again, don't wrap the hackle's stem up against the wings; leave just the tiniest space so as to preserve the wings' position.

4. When tying off a hackle tip, I find it easiest to hold the tip firmly over the hook and tipped slightly forward.

5. Learn to release the hackle's tip from the pliers without breaking it or pulling it about. It can help to use both hands for this.

6. If the wings have gone astray, tug them back into position.

### WRAPPING DRY FLY HACKLES

**12.** Wrap one hackle forward in small spirals and secure its tip under thread turns.

**13.** Wrap the other hackle through the spaces of the first and secure its tip.

**14.** Snip both hackles' tips and complete the fly.

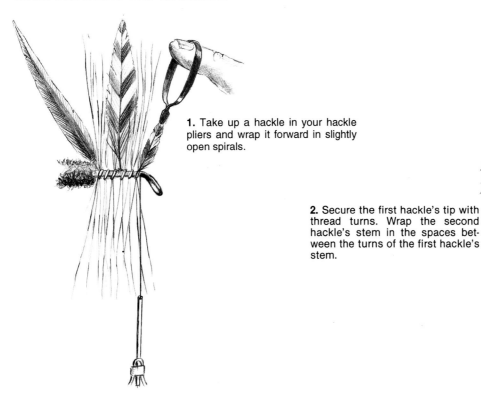

**1.** Take up a hackle in your hackle pliers and wrap it forward in slightly open spirals.

**2.** Secure the first hackle's tip with thread turns. Wrap the second hackle's stem in the spaces between the turns of the first hackle's stem.

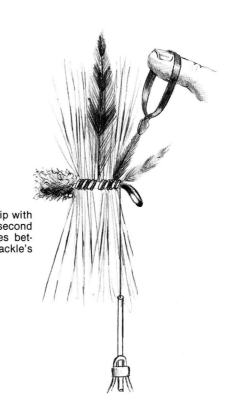

# More Classic Dry Fly Wings And Bodies

**1.** Whether it is peacock herl or hackle, remove the fibers from the quill (stem). (The method shown is for herl only.)

**2.** Wrap the quill (or stem) up the shank, secure it, and trim it.

**3.** When the fly is finished, add head cement to the body (especially with herl quills.)

DUCK QUILL WINGS

**1.** Cut sections from a matched pair of duck quills.

**2.** Take up the sections, tips curving apart and evened, in your left hand.

## The Quill Body

In this category I include both the stripped peacock-quill and stripped hackle-stem types. I group them together both because they are constructed in the same manner, and because stems are often referred to as quills. Let's begin with the stripped peacock quill.

Strip the fibers from the quill with either your thumbnail or a pencil eraser—the thumbnail is simply scraped up the quill (against the grain of the fibers); the eraser is stroked along the quill (same direction) on a flat surface. I now prefer the eraser method after having once embedded a bit of broken quill into the soft (and I can assure you, tender) skin beneath my thumbnail. Thoroughly strip the quill on both sides.

Dampen the quill to reduce its brittleness, Tie it in by the last 1/4 inch or so at the bend (of course, the wings and tail are already tied in). Wrap the quill, in close turns, up the shank to the rear of the hackle area. Secure the quill's end with thread turns and then trim it. Peacock quills are fragile, so add a thin layer of head cement over the quill body when you cement the thread head.

The second quill body—the hackle stem—is constructed in about the same manner as was the peacock-quill body; the differences are that hackle stems are stripped differently than are peacock quills and the fact that hackle stems may not require a coating of head cement, though it is optional. Because hackle stems are thin, large hooks may require two for a body. Simply wrap both at the same time.

## Duck Quill Wings

More quill confusion: here "quill" refers to the fibers of a primary wing flight feather. Begin with the two layers of thread as you did with the Adams. Select a pair of matched duck quills ("matched" in this case means they are similar in form and hue, but come from opposite wings—mirror images). Cut a section about 1/8 inch wide from the same part of each quill. Put the sections back to back, long edges down, tips evened, between the first finger and thumb of your left hand. Measure the sections against the hook as you did the hackle-tip wings for the Adams, and then tie in the sections using the pinch. Cut the butts of the quills at an angle in preparation for adding the tails and body.

A few pointers on this pinch are in order. Since you have two flat, fairly fragile sections that must be compressed in one direction only, the pinch must be particularly well executed. One thing that will help is to lower your pinch thumb and finger down the sides of the hook shank slightly as you close the thread loop; you can also roll the thumb and finger tips forward at the same time. Drawing the thread slightly towards you, instead of straight down, also helps. Once the loop is tight, hold the thread taught as you add the securing thread turns.

You will have to be aggressive as you set the wings upright (after the body and tails are finished of course). If you pinch the wings flatly as you pursue this, their flatness should be preserved. (If the wings are really resisting an upright set, press your thumbnail in hard at their base to give them a strong crease; more on this can be found in this section under "Setting the Wings and Tying in the Hackles—Problems, Solutions, and Suggestions" and in "The Gray Wulff" under "Setting the Wings and Hackling.") Build a thread dam in front of the wings as you did for the Adams. The debate remains as to whether or not the thread should pass between the wings. Figure-eight thread turns from one edge of the wings to the other help divide the wings, and if you run the thread around each wing, as we will for wood-duck wings, it can help set them upright securely. For now, don't run the thread between the wings; but later, when all seems to be going smoothly, you might want to try figure-eight wing wraps on duck quill sections.

## Wood Duck Wings

Wood-duck wings are delicately barred; they are really quite lovely; it is no wonder they are so often used on classic dry flies. Because wood-duck feathers are often scarce and usually expensive, mallard feathers dyed wood-duck color are often substituted.

Begin with the two thread layers as usual. Strip the fuzz from the base of a single wood-duck feather, and then strip one 3/16 inch section from each side of the stem. If the tips of the sections are not squared on the feather, you can square them by drawing the sections to a right angle to the stem (or whatever angle works) before stripping them.

Set the sections back to back between the first finger and thumb of your left hand, and then tie them in using the pinch, as you did the duck-quill wings. For fuller wood-duck wings, add a second pair outside the first; simply set the second pair flanking the first, and then tie them in with the pinch.

Once the tail and body are complete, lift the wings and support them with a thread dam. Now turn your head so that you are sighting straight down the front of the hook. Note the curve of the fibers's tips; tips that curve to the far side will make up the far-side wing and tips curving to the near side, near-side wings. Separate the wings into their appropriate sides with the closed tips of your scissors' blades. Grasp the far-side fibers flatly, and tug them firmly to that side; do the same with the near-side fibers, but to the near side. Bring the thread up, and then back so that it angles from the front of the near wing to the back of the far wing. Wind the thread under the shank and then up again. Run the thread from the *rear* of the near wing to the *front* of the far wing—now the wings are really divided.

Bring the thread between the wings again to their rear. Take two turns around the shank, and then bring the thread forward between the wings again, but instead of wrapping the thread around the shank, wind the thread around the far wing only. This will bring the thread around the outside of the wing; the thread-winding direction has now been reversed. Lift the wing flatly and sharply upright, pull the thread tightly towards you and back to support the wing upright, release the wing and add three tight turns of thread around the shank. Repeat this process with the near wing. With that, both wings are solidly upright and the thread direction is back to normal. Save leftover wood-duck feather tips, as these can be matched and used for wings.

### SETTING WOOD-DUCK WINGS

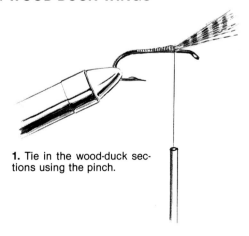

**1.** Tie in the wood-duck sections using the pinch.

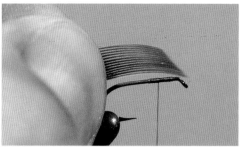

**3.** Measure the sections against the hook.

**4.** Tie in the sections using the pinch. Snip the sections' butts at an angle.

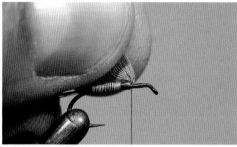

**5.** Add the tail and body (shown is a hackle-stem body), and then pull the wings firmly back as you build thread turns at the base of the wings.

**6.** Properly set wings; next comes hackles.

WOOD DUCK WINGS

**1.** Wood-duck feathers, one stripped, and one with a set of wing sections removed. If necessary, adjust a section to square its tips before you strip it from the stem.

**2.** Tie in the sections using the pinch.

**3.** Add the tail and body. Lift the wings, as you did the duck quills, and support them with thread. Sight down the front of the wings and divide the fibers.

**4.** Draw the wing groups to the sides and work the thread through them in figure-eights.

**5.** Draw the wings up, one at a time, with a turn of thread.

**6.** A properly set pair of wood-duck wings.

## SETTING WOOD-DUCK WINGS CONTINUED

**2.** Pull the wood-duck sections sharply back and build thread turns at their base.

**3.** Sight down the front of the wood-duck fibers and divide them into two groups with the tips of your scissors. Pull the groups firmly to the sides.

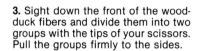

**4.** Pass the thread from the front of the near wing to the rear of the far wing.

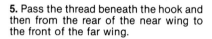

**5.** Pass the thread beneath the hook and then from the rear of the near wing to the front of the far wing.

**6.** Pass the thread beneath the hook and then from the front of the near wing to the rear of the far wing again. Add two thread turns just behind the wings. Pass the thread from the rear of the near wing to the front of the far wing again; **then, pass the thread around the outside of the far wing and then over the top of the hook and down the near side.** Thread direction is now reversed.

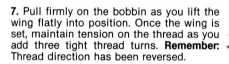

**7.** Pull firmly on the bobbin as you lift the wing flatly into position. Once the wing is set, maintain tension on the thread as you add three tight thread turns. **Remember:** Thread direction has been reversed.

**8.** Pass the thread between the wings again and then around the near wing. Raise and set the near wing as you did the far one. Now the thread is back to its original direction.

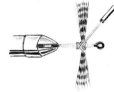

**9.** The wings are set; hackles next.

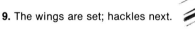

# GRAY WULFF

The Adams was designed for lazy currents and modest riffles; the Gray Wulff is sort of a rough-water Adams—the hair wing and tail make the difference.

Lee Wulff, American fly-fishing writer, innovator, fly designer—truly a fly-fishing legend—devised a whole series of hair-wing, hair-tail dry flies with names ending in "Wulff." The Wulff series may well be his most widely recognized accomplishment, and one fly in this series is the Gray Wulff.

Here you will learn to handle hair wings and tail; nothing drastically different from traditional dry flies, but some new techniques are in order.

Fish the Gray Wulff—or any of the "Wulffs" as they are often called—in streams too broken and turbulent for traditional dry flies. Fish it dead drift, or make it dance if that seems appropriate. Large Wulffs are often fished for steelhead and Atlantic salmon, but mostly, they are fished for trout.

## GRAY WULFF

**Hook:** Any dry-fly hook, sizes 16 to 8.
**Thread:** Black, 8/0 or 6/0.
**Wings And Tail:** Brown bucktail.
**Body:** Gray dubbing.
**Hackle:** Blue dun.

**Note:** Lee is quite open-minded regarding materials for his Wulff series—calf tail or even elk hair could be used for the wings and tail, and yarn could be used for the body. But the dressing listed here is the one I see most often.

## Tying In The Wings And Tail

Begin by sizing two blue-dun dry fly hackles. Smash the barb on a standard size-10 dry-fly hook (the hook shown is a Gamakatsu model No. F13), and mount it in your vise. Lay down a two-layer thread base as you did for the Adams. Cut a bunch of brown bucktail and draw out the short fibers. You can hand stack the bucktail, as you did for the Mickey Finn, or you can use a hair-stacking tool. The brown fibers that form a streak down the center of a bucktail (these are the ones you will use here) behave well in a hair stacker, but the white outside fibers do not, as they tend to clump together and resist the tapping of the stacker—especially if they are dyed (which is why the wing of the Mickey Finn was entirely hand stacked). The best way to stack hair for average to small trout flies is in a hair-stacking tool, usually called a "hair stacker."

Here is how to use a hair stacker. Drop the bunch of bucktail tip first into the stacker. With your thumb or fingertip over its opening, tap the stacker a few times down onto a hard surface (covering the opening is optional—insurance that the hairs won't go flying should you get carried away with your tapping). Turn the stacker on its side, remove its cap, and remove the stacked hairs by their tips. If you handle the hairs carefully and deliberately, their tips will stay even.

1. Snip a bunch of bucktail hair and place it tip first into a hair stacker.

**2.** Tap the stacker a few times on a hard surface.

**3.** Remove the stacker's cap, and then remove the hair bunch.

**4.** Measure and then tie in the hair bunch using the pinch.

**5A.** Trim the hairs' butts at an angle and bind them with thread.

**ANGLE CUT HAIR BUTTS**

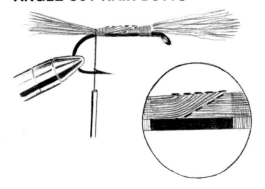

Measure the stacked fibers against the hook, and then tie them in using the pinch (same length as all dry-fly wings we've covered thus far). Add plenty of tight securing thread turns to adjust for the fibers's bulk, stiffness, and slickness; work these turns toward the bend until the wing is secured with a tight thread collar about 1/8 inch long. Trim the butts of the fibers by lifting them, and then cutting them at an angle. Bind the trimmed butt ends under thread wraps. Stack another bunch of bucktail about half the size of the first. With the thread at the last 1/4 of the shank before the bend, measure and then tie in the tails using the pinch. Bind the tails tightly with securing thread turns. Lift the butts of the tail fibers and snip them at an angle. Bind the trimmed butt ends under thread wraps, then lift the tails, and work the thread down them to the bend.

## Tying In The Wings And Tail — Problems, Solutions, And Suggestions

1. Gentle taps are all that is required to stack hair.

2. Applying the pinch several times is a good way to secure the wing hair, control it, and keep it on top of the hook.

3. Determining the correct amount of hair for the wings and tail is a bit tricky, since there is no stem or flat section to measure. Overly thick wings and tail become unruly to tie with and give the fly an unnatural appearance; overly thin ones offer insufficient buoyancy — proper wing and tail density is worth some attention. Perhaps the best answer is simply to study the photos and, though some stylistic leeway is fine, use them as a guide.

4. Though I've already said it, lots of tight thread turns to hold in the wing hairs really help make the tying of the Gray Wulff go smoothly. It's worth repeating.

5. If the thread keeps breaking when securing the hair wings and tail, start with 3/0 thread and then switch to 8/0 or 6/0 after the wings and tail are secured.

6. Try to make the angle cuts at the butts of the wing hairs and tail hairs such that they blend into a smoothly tapered body; a smooth foundation makes smooth application of materials easiest — this is true of fly tying in general.

## Setting The Wings And Hackling

Dub the body as usual (the dubbing pictured is poly dubbing). Be aggressive in pulling the wings upright — the stiff hairs are resistant to bending. Get your right-hand thumbnail right down at the base of the hairs, and then roll your nail back firmly against them to crease them; repeat this at the sides of the hairs as well. Once the hairs seem to be taking on the crease, pull them sharply back and add some tight thread turns at their base to support them upright. Sight down the front of the fly, and use your scissors' tips to separate the clump of hairs into two equal wing groups (see "Wood Duck Wings" under "The Adams and the Classic Dry Fly"). Tug the groups sharply to the sides of the hook. Work the thread to just behind the wings. Make a few figure-eight thread turns between the wings. From here, proceed to set the wings upright just as you did for the wood-duck wings, although taking two thread turns around each wing before setting it upright will really help to group its fibers. You may also need to use more thread pressure on the bucktail than the wood duck required.

Tie in the hackles, and then wrap them as you did for the Adams. Complete the fly as usual.

## Setting The Wings And Hackling—
## Problems, Solutions, And Suggestions

1. As with tails, the tightness of the thread around the wings will determine how much they flare; just how much they should flare is largely a matter of personal taste—the point is that you can control the degree of flare in hair wings.

2. Because of its stiff hairs, each wing may require that you set it upright with a tight, angled-back turn of thread more than once; just keep adding these turns until the wing really stands up.

3. Since this is a rough-water fly, some tiers start the hackle slightly farther back on the shank than they would for classic flies, and squeeze an extra turn or two out of each hackle by stripping less butt fibers and wrapping more of the hackle's tip. The use of long rooster saddle hackles can also add more hackle. Another option is to use three hackles; to do this, simply leave a bit more space between turns of the first hackle and wrap the remaining two hackles, one at a time, in this space.

The hair wings and tail account for the main difference in buoyancy between the Wulff flies and classic dry flies; the amount of hackle you use is up to you.

Frank Amato Photo

**5B.** Stack and tie in a smaller hair bunch for a tail. Trim the butts of these hairs at an angle and bind them with thread.

**6.** Dub the body. Crease the wing hair upright with your thumbnail.

**7.** Divide the wing hair into two equal groups and tug the groups sharply apart.

**8.** With thread, separate the groups and set each upright.

**9.** Tie in and wind the hackles.

# ELK HAIR CADDIS

The word "ingenious" is occasionally used to describe fly patterns. This is usually because the fly has some tying wrinkle that simplifies and improves the fly. By this definition, Al Troth's Elk Hair Caddis is ingenious indeed.

Al found a way to slant the hackle back—a big benefit for a caddis imitation, since these are often twitched and skidded across the surface—and to reinforce the hackle with the same fine wire that secures it.

The Elk Hair Caddis can be fished dead drift, with an occasional twitch, or really made to dance and struggle.

### ELK HAIR CADDIS

**Hook:** Standard dry fly, sizes 18 to 8.
**Thread:** Tan 3/0.
**Rib:** Fine gold wire.
**Body:** Hare's mask dubbing.
**Hackle:** Brown.
**Wing:** Bleached elk hair.

## The Rib, Body, And Hackle

Begin by sizing a single No. 12 dry-fly hackle. Smash the barb on a standard size-12 dry-fly hook (the hook shown is a Tiemco model 100), and mount it in your vise. Start the thread about 1/16 inch behind the eye. Use a light turn to tie in the wire, and then secure it with tight thread turns. Lift the wire slightly above the shank, under light tension, and spiral the thread down it to the bend. Add a few tight securing thread turns here. Dub the shank fairly heavily up to 1/16 inch behind the eye. If the wire remains on the spool, trim it a few inches from the hook.

Tie in the hackle about 1/8" behind the eye, and then trim its stem. Spiral (palmer) the hackle back to the bend in six to ten turns. When the hackle reaches the bend, hold the hackle pliers up and slightly back from the bend in your left hand. Grasp the wire in your right hand, and make one tight turn over the hackle's tip. Keep tension on the wire with your right hand as you release the hackle pliers with your left. Add three more turns of wire over the tip, and then spiral the wire forward through the hackle. When the wire reaches a point 1/8 inch behind the eye, tie it off with thread, add a few tight, securing thread turns, and trim the wire. Trim the hackle's tip.

The winding of hackle and wire is all in the standard direction.

## The Rib, Body, And Hackle— Problems, Solutions, And Suggestions

1. The gold wire becomes fragile if kinked—and especially fragile if a loop tightens into a knot or fold. So handle the wire carefully.

**1.** Tie in gold wire and dub the body.

2. It helps to tie the wire off (after it has been wound through the hackle) on top of the hook; this way, the wing will later hide its end.

3. If you have trouble with the complications of holding the hackle pliers up as you secure the hackle's tip with the wire, simply let the pliers hang when the hackle reaches the bend; then work the wire around the hanging tip and pliers. The pliers-up method, however, makes for a neater fly and an easier time trimming the hackle's tip later.

## The Wing

Snip a small bunch of elk hair from its hide. Hold the hair by its tips as you stroke a comb through it to remove the short hairs and fuzz. That is how you comb hair; any comb with fairly fine teeth will do. Stack the hair in a hair stacker. Measure the hair against the hook; to do this, set the tips of the hair about 1/8 to 3/16 inch beyond the rear extremity of the hook's bend, and then snip the butts straight across at the tip of the eye. Set the hair bunch on top of the hook with the tips rearward and the trimmed butts at the very rear of the eye. Tie in the hair bunch here using the pinch. Add several tight securing turns of thread to form a collar. At this point, the tips of the hair should sweep back over the body, and the butts should flare a bit just in front of the thread collar which is just behind the eye. Add a triple whip finish, trim the thread, and add head cement to the collar.

## The Wing— Problems, Solutions, And Suggestions

1. Check the photographs to determine the proper amount of wing hair.

2. A really tight collar is good insurance against having the wing roll and so is a well-executed pinch in which the thumb and finger really keep the hairs on top of the shank.

3. Use the pinch more than once if the wing keeps trying to roll around the shank.

4. Careful measuring of the wing is important—a stubby or too-long wing makes the Elk Hair Caddis an unconvincing imitation.

2. Tie in a dry-fly hackle.

3. Palmer the hackle down the body to the bend.

4. Tie off the hackle's tip with the gold wire.

5. Spiral wire forward through hackle. Secure end of wire with thread turns and trim wire's end.

6. Comb and stack a bunch of elk hair and then measure it against the hook.

7. Hold the hair over the hook and snip it cleanly just in front of the hook's eye.

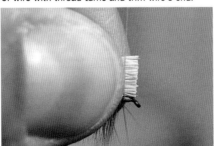

8. Move the bunch back so that its blunt end is just behind the eye; then tie it in using the pinch.

9. Build a tight thread collar, whip finish and trim thread, and add head cement to thread collar.

# COMPARADUN (MARCH BROWN)

In *Comparahatch*, published in 1972, Al Caucci and Bob Nastasi introduced fly fishers to a remarkably simple and effective fly: the Comparadun. Where once the Adams and other classic dry-fly patterns were every angler's first choice now this relative newcomer stands on equal ground. The March Brown version listed is only a sample; the Comparadun is tied in many colors to imitate many species of mayflies.

The Comparadun wing makes the Comparadun—it is a fan of deer hair that simulates the natural's wings and legs. Split tails are becoming commonplace on mayfly imitations, and you will learn to handle these in tying the Comparadun too.

For mayfly hatches in slow to moderate currents, fish the Comparadun dead drift or with the slightest twitches if appropriate.

## COMPARADUN (MARCH BROWN)

**Hook:** Standard dry fly, sizes 14 to 10. (Comparaduns other than this March Brown version range from 24 to 10.)
**Thread:** 8/0 or 6/0 tan.
**Wing:** Brown natural coastal deer hair.
**Tail:** Brown hackle fibers.
**Abdomen And Thorax:** Tan dubbing.

## Tying In The Wing And Tail

Smash the barb on a standard dry-fly hook, size 14, and mount it in your vise (the hook shown is an Eagle Claw model D59). Start the thread about 1/16 inch behind the eye, and then wrap a double thread layer exactly as you did for the Adams. Snip a bunch of coastal deer hair from its hide; the exact amount is difficult to describe, so use the photographs for reference. Comb and stack the hair (if handled carefully, this hair may not need stacking; its tips are quite even when still on the hide). By the sound of it, one might assume that coastal deer hair could only be obtained through close friendship with a coastal-deer hunter; but obscure though it once was, coastal deer hair is now carried by most fly shops and mail-order houses. I specify "coastal" because many other types of deer hair are too spongy for Comparadun wings.

Measure the wing so that it is the full length of the hook, and then tie it in using the pinch. Secure it well with tight thread turns. With the first finger of your left hand, push the wing down around the hook as you make a few tight thread turns forward about 1/16 inch—this will help properly distribute the hairs later. Lift the hair butts, cut them at an angle, bind their cut ends with thread, and then spiral the thread to the bend.

This method for creating split tails is my own, though it is similar to the one described in *Comparahatch*. Make about eight to twelve turns at the bend until a small thread ball is formed. Advance the thread up about

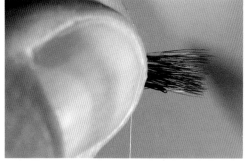

1. Build a layer of thread; comb, stack, measure; then tie in a bunch of deer hair.

1/4 of the shank. Strip about 1/4 inch of fibers from a brown dry-fly hackle, measure them against the hook, and then use the pinch to tie them in at midshank so that they extend about one full hook's length beyond the bend. Lift the fibers as you wind the thread down them; stop when about three consecutive thread turns remain to reach the thread ball. Pull the tail fibers down firmly around the ball; some fibers will remain on top while others will slip around the sides. Wrap the last few turns of thread firmly to the front of the ball. Release the tail fibers; they should now splay out from around the top half of the thread ball.

**2.** Push the wing down around the hook and add a few more tight thread turns.

## Tying In The Wing And Tail— Problems, Solutions, And Suggestions

1. If you choose to leave the hair unstacked, draw it first to a right angle to the hide, stroke your grip down the hair to even the tension, and then grip the hair firmly as you snip it free of the hide. After that, handle it carefully to keep the tips even.

2. Two tricks will help you tie in the wing securely: Start with 3/0 thread and then switch to 8/0 or 6/0 after the wing is in; run the thread back to the bare shank now and then as you bind the wing's butt—Richard Bunse refers to the bare-shank wraps as "anchoring" wraps.

3. If the wing rolls around the shank as you wrap forward over it, try making light-tension turns, and then pressing up from beneath the shank with a finger as each turn is pulled tight. Another way is to pull the hair forward by its tips with your right hand as you work the bobbin over the hair and pull each turn tight with your left.

4. To lift the hair butts, slide your right-hand thumb and first finger down beneath the shank, pinch the thumb and finger together, and then draw them up as the shank slips between them and they catch and raise the hair butts for trimming.

5. Angling the thread back and forth across the thread ball can help you form it with ease—and be certain you add all the thread-ball turns in one spot.

**3.** Snip the hair butts at an angle, bind them with thread, and build a thread ball at the bend.

## Dubbing, Setting The Wing Upright, And Snipping The Split Tails

Trim the butts of the hackle fibers. Spin some dubbing onto the thread (rabbit fur is pictured, but any dubbing is fine). Dub a tapered body from the tails to the rear of the wing. Place your right-hand thumbnail over the eye, right under the wing. Slide your thumbnail to the base of the wing as you roll the first joint of your thumb upward. Press back against the wing as you roll the first joint of your thumb right over the wing and really force the wing upright. This is essentially the same motion you used to crease the Gray Wulff's wing upright. Repeat this motion on both sides of the wing. The wing should now form a fan around the top half of the fly.

Draw the wing sharply back and take a turn of dubbing in front of it. Continue this turn of dubbing to the far side of the hook, and then bring it back under and to the rear of the wing; you will have to release the wing now. Bring the dubbing back under the wing and to the front of it again—you are crisscrossing the dubbing beneath the wing to gather the wing hairs and cover the wing's underside.

Draw back the wing again and add a few tight turns of dubbing right up against it to really set the wing upright. Continue dubbing to the rear

**4.** Tie in some hackle fibers and wrap back over them with thread; nearing the thread ball, pull the fibers down around it and add the final turns of thread.

**5.** Dub to the wing, and then crease the wing upright, once on top and once on each side.

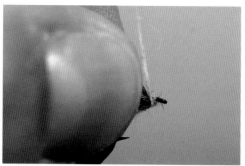

**6.** Draw the wing sharply back and take a turn of dubbing up against the front of its base.

**7.** Crisscross the dubbing beneath the wing. Add more dubbing in front of the wing and complete the head as usual.

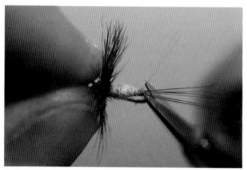

**8.** Snip the center fibers from the tail, leaving split tails.

**9.** Split tails.

of the head area, create a thread head, add a triple whip finish, trim the thread and add head cement.

The final step (although it can be performed before the head is cemented) is to trim the tails. To do this slip your open scissors' blades up into the tail right at the bend so that two to four fibers lay outside the blades on each side. Snip. Now the center fibers are gone, and all that remains are two bunches of outside fibers—split tails. You can use all the snips you need in order to accomplish this, but eventually you will hone them down to one efficient snip.

## Dubbing, Setting The Wings Upright, And Snipping The Split Tails— Problems, Solutions, And Suggestions

1. The wing hairs may rotate too far down the sides of the hook; use the crisscrossed turns of dubbing to draw these hairs up into the rest of the wing. Again, the wing should be a half-circle, a fan, around the top of the fly.

2. The distribution of hairs in the wing is a good indication of how the wing was tied in—if the hairs are clumped at the center, you need to push the wing down around the hook more as you secure it with thread turns.

3. An even more secure way to set the wing upright is to use lots of tight turns of bare thread against the front of the wing; then dub around and beneath the wing to the head area.

4. Another way to snip the tail fibers is to leave the fly in the vise, and then pull some outside fibers toward you to separate them from the rest for clear access with your scissor tips.

# LIGHT CAHILL PARACHUTE

The original Light Cahill existed well before the Light Cahill Parachute; this is the case with many of the parachute flies. The term "parachute" comes from the manner in which the hackle is wound: horizontally, above the hook, truly creating a sort of parachute appearance and effect. The parachute-style fly was designed to give better visibility to the angler in bad-light situations with small dry flies.

Most dry flies can be tied parachute style. The Light Cahill is a good example of typical parachute adaptation—the original pair of wings is replaced with a single hair wing which is set slightly farther forward; all of which is to accommodate the hackle. However, I have seen parachutes with almost every type of wing imaginable: duck-quill sections, poly yarn, mallard-breast feathers cut to wing shape—anything that will provide an adequate foundation for the hackle. There are really no hard rules about parachutes.

The benefits of the parachute style are that the position of the hackle really helps the fly alight upright and that the hackle fibers radiate around the thorax as do the legs of most trout-stream insects. Parachutes are a bit tricky to tie, but only a bit, and they are worth the effort. The Light Cahill Parachute is a mayfly imitation. Fish it dead drift.

## LIGHT CAHILL PARACHUTE

**Hook:** Standard dry fly, sizes 18 to 10.
**Thread:** 8/0 or 6/0, tan.
**Wing:** A single bunch of white calf tail.
**Tail:** Ginger hackle fibers.
**Hackle:** Ginger
**Body:** Badger underfur.

## Tying In The Wing, Tail, And Hackle

Select and size a No. 12 dry-fly hackle. Start the thread about 1/16 inch back from the eye of a size-12 dry-fly hook (the hook shown is a Partridge Grey Shadow model GRS3A). Wrap the thread to just short of mid-shank, and then wrap it forward to just *past* (not just short of, as with the Adams) the middle of the first thread layer. Comb and stack a bunch of calf tail. Measure the calf tail against the hook (some tiers prefer a slightly shorter-than-usual wing on parachute flies). Tie in the calf tail using the pinch; add several tight securing turns of thread. Trim the hair butts at an angle.

Lift the wing firmly upright, and then crease it with a firm press from your right-hand thumbnail (see "Setting The Wings Upright" under "The Gray Wulff"). Wrap up the base of the hair wing with *light-tension* thread turns; the thread wraps should be counter clockwise. When the thread is *at least* 1/16 inch up the wing, wind the thread back down the wing. Draw the thread sharply and firmly back to really hold the wing upright, and then secure the thread in several tight turns (see "Wood Duck Wings" under "The Adams"); repeat this step if required to really set the wing upright.

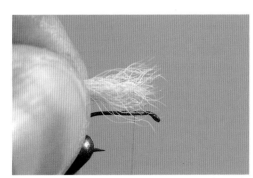

1. Lay down a double thread layer; then cut, comb, stack, measure, and tie in a bunch of calf tail.

**2.** Pull the hair back and crease it upright with your thumbnail.

**3.** Secure the hair wing's upright position with thread; then wrap thread up and down the base of the wing.

**4.** Prepare and then tie in a hackle against the base of the wing. Run the thread up and down the wing's base again, covering the hackle stem as well.

**5.** Draw the stem of the hackle back along the shank; secure the stem with thread, trim it, and cover its cut end and the hair butts with thread.

**6.** Dub from the bend to just in front of the wing.

Prepare the hackle and then hold it against the thread-wound base of the wings; the hackle should be vertical, on the near side of the hook, curve toward you, bare stem ending just past the top of the thread wraps on the wing. Tie the hackle onto the wing base using a light turn around the wing and hackle stem only, instead of around the shank as usual. Wrap the thread, under more tension this time, up the base of the wing, securing the hackle at the same time. Wind the thread back down to the shank. You now have a solid foundation for the winding of the hackle. Draw the remaining hackle-stem butt so that it lies along the shank. Wrap the thread down the shank and butt 1/16 to 1/8 inch, add a few securing thread turns and trim the hackle stem.

Measure and then tie in the tails just as you did for the Adams, except that these tails are all one color and therefore are all mounted with one pinch.

## Tying In The Wing, Tail, And Hackle — Problems, Solutions, And Suggestions

1. A thorough combing really helps the stacking of kinky calf-tail fibers. You can comb it on the hide, or after it has been cut.

2. Really set the wing upright; a firm thumbnail crease and solid thread support will do it. The angle of the wing will determine the angle of the parachute hackle later—if the wing tips sit forward then so will the hackle, but a vertical wing will create a neatly horizontal hackle.

3. Some tiers tie the hackle onto the shank, and then wind it up and then back down the wing. But to me this is a shortcut—winding the hackle stem onto the wing adds support, and rather than crisscrossing itself as it would if tied in only at the shank, the hackle winds neatly in consecutive turns down the wing. If this doesn't quite make sense now, it will soon—the point is that I request that you give my approach a chance before you let someone else talk you into an "easier way."

4. Grasp the wing firmly, as needed, to support it as you tighten the thread around it.

5. You can hold the wing throughout the wrapping of its base. Simply drop the bobbin down the far side after each turn, and then reach around from behind the wing to retrieve the bobbin for the next turn. Eventually, however, you will find that the less you hold the wing, the faster you'll complete this step.

6. The ideal way to create a parachute wing and prepare its base for the hackle (at least the best way I've found) is to wrap the first layer of thread up the wing's base under light tension (this gathers the fibers); the next layer goes back down under more tension; from here each layer of thread can be tighter than the previous one because every layer (and the hackle's stem) adds stiffness—this way, you may never have to hold the wing as you thread wrap it.

7. For insurance that your wing won't later roll to one side, set it upright with the thread tightly drawn back and secured on one side of the hook, and then repeat this with the thread drawn back and secured on the *other* side of the hook. It is best to use the side that reverses thread-winding direction first, so that the next side reestablishes the original direction.

## Dubbing And Hackling

Snip some cream-colored badger fur from its hide. Hold the tips of the guard hairs firmly, and then draw out the soft fuzz from around the cut ends of the hairs; this fuzz will be your dubbing. Wax the thread, if you choose, and then spin on the dubbing and dub up the shank to 1/16 inch behind the eye. This, of course, means that you will dub in front of the wing a bit.

Lock the tip of the hackle in your hackle pliers. Wrap the hackle counterclockwise in close turns down the thread-wrapped base of the wing. When the hackle reaches the body (about four to six turns of hackle), lower the pliers down the far side of the shank and let them hang.

Place your left-hand thumb, first, and second fingers around the front of the hackle and draw the fibers up and back from the head area in a sort of modified triangle. Secure the hackle tip with tight thread turns. Release the bobbin from your right hand, take up the scissors in it and snip off the hackle's tip. Regrasp the bobbin in your right hand and create a thread head. Add a triple whip finish. Coat the head with cement. Later, when the cement is fully hardened, you can tug the hackle and wing back to their original position (the modified triangle leaves the hackle and wing kicked back).

## Dubbing And Hackling— Problems, Solutions, And Suggestions

1. An extra turn or two of the dubbing, angled from the front of the wing back and then from behind the wing forward helps to cover the lower sides of the wing.

2. Feel free to grasp the wing as needed for support as you wrap the hackle. It can help to grasp the wing after each turn as you pull the hackle snug, although ideally you need never support the wing after it's set upright, and in fact this goal is quite obtainable.

3. Keep the hackle turns next to one another; spreading them out allows for less turns of hackle.

4. When you use the modified triangle, don't use excessive force or you might slide the hackle off the wing—especially if the hackles tip is not yet fully secured under a thread-head.

5. When adding the whip finish, it helps to slip the loop low over the thread-head, beneath the hackles.

**7.** Wrap the hackle down the thread-wrapped base of the wing in close, consecutive turns. When you can wrap the hackle no farther, let your hackle pliers hang on the far side of the hook in front of the wing.

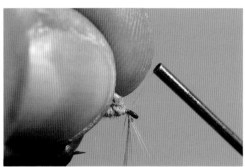

**8.** Draw back the hackle fibers in a modified triangle, and secure the hackle's tip with tight thread turns. Release the bobbin, trim the hackle's tip, build a thread head, add a triple whip finish, coat the head with head cement.

**9.** Once the head cement is hard you can tug the wing and hackle back into shape.

**10.** Note how the hackle fibers radiate from the wing on the finished parachute.

# GRIFFITH'S GNAT

Were you to judge the difficulty of tying the Griffith's Gnat by its pattern, it would seem that this fly would be the first we tie rather than the last. But the catch is in the size, which is small indeed. This size 18 hook is tiny, and it will test you a bit. But a size 18 hook is hardly small for the Griffith's Gnat; it is often tied on hooks as tiny as size 22, 24, and even 26 and smaller (though I've never fished a fly smaller than size 24). The tying-sequence photographs show the jaws of a special tiny-fly vise called a "Spartan," but for perspective, the photograph of the finished Griffith's Gnat shows the jaws of the same much-used Renzetti vise shown with all the other flies.

Every experienced trout angler today knows that tiny flies are often critical to success, and that fish frequently feed on tiny insects to the exclusion of all else. Heavy feeding on tiny flies was only a few decades ago considered a fine time for an angler's nap; it is now considered a time for fine sport.

Here are a few pointers that will help you tie the Griffith's Gnat or any tiny fly. Strong lighting becomes more important than ever when tying tiny; if you have a lever-arm lamp, bring it down close to your work. Magnification is important here; magnifying glasses, capable of at least triple magnification, help tremendously, as do arm-mounted magnifiers. Use materials sparingly.—two to four turns of hackle are usually plenty on conventional hackle-collar dry flies, dubbing should be barely enough to cover the thread, and keep turns of thread to a minimum. More than ever, adequate room must be left for a thread head. Wings, ribs, and nymph legs are often considered optional on really tiny dry flies—when everything gets this small, trout seem to pay less attention to detail. Finally, slow down—a modest pace and the willingness to take some extra time at a problem spot will ensure that your tiny tying is effective and enjoyable.

The Griffith's Gnat imitates a tiny fly called a "midge," that is half-free of its pupal shuck. Fish the Griffith's Gnat dead drift and half sunk; one way to accomplish this is to apply floatant to the top half of the fly only. George Griffith created this fly.

## GRIFFITH'S GNAT

**Hook:** Light-wire, sizes 18 and smaller.
**Thread:** 8/0 olive, gray, or black.
**Hackle:** Grizzly, dry fly.
**Body:** Peacock herl.

**1.** Tie in the peacock herl, then the hackle.

## Tying The Griffith's Gnat

First you must size a hackle. This can be accomplished easily enough for a size 18 hook, but hackles for hook sizes smaller than 22 are difficult to size on a hackle gauge. For this reason, and because I find it much easier to hand size hackles for tiny hooks than for larger ones, I simply wrap a hackle once around the hook to determine appropriateness.

Once your hackle is selected, smash the barb on a size-18 dry-fly hook (the hook shown is a Mustad, model 94859) and mount it in your vise. Start the thread a short space behind the eye and spiral it to the bend. Strip the stem of the hackle and tie in the stem at the bend. Trim the stem closely (after a few securing thread turns) or lift the stem, advance the thread to its tie-in point, lower the stem, secure the stem using the pinch, and trim its end—you decide. Either way, the hackle is tied in, its stem is trimmed, and the thread is advanced to its tie-in point.

Tie in a quill of peacock herl, add securing thread turns, raise the quill and spiral the thread down it, and the shank, to the bend; trim the end of the peacock.

Wrap the peacock quill up the shank in close turns. Secure its end with thread, trim the projecting quill. Palmer (spiral) the hackle up the peacock body in four to six turns. Tie off the hackle tip, trim it closely, create a tiny thread head, and add a triple whip finish and head cement.

**2.** Wrap the peacock herl, secure it with thread turns, trim it.

## Tying The Griffith's Gnat — Problems, Solutions, And Suggestions

1. Select the peacock herl by the length of its fibers—the shortest-fibered quills are appropriate for the tiniest hooks.

2. The fibers of the hackle and quill can sweep forward or back—a matter of personal preference (if you are tying with magnification, you will especially notice that herl fibers cup just as do hackle fibers).

3. Wrapping the herl and hackle tightly without breaking them is trickier here than usual—take your time, and keep developing your feel.

4. The triangle can be tough to execute on tiny flies. A modified version of the triangle can be performed with only the thumb and first finger; these two can effectively cover the whole head of such a tiny fly. A bit of moisture will also help drawn-back materials stay clear of the eye as you form the thread head.

**3.** Palmer the hackle down the herl body; finish the fly as usual.

Frank Amato Photo

# ADDITIONAL NYMPHS

## 1. BLACK WOOLLY WORM

**Hook:** Heavy wire, 2X to 3X long, sizes 14 to 2.
**Thread:** Black 8/0, 6/0, or 3/0.
**Tail:** Red hackle fibers.
**Hackle:** Grizzly.
**Body:** Black chenille.

## 2. BOX CANYON STONE
*Mims Barker*

**Hook:** Heavy wire, 2X to 4X long, sizes 10 to 8.
**Thread:** Black 8/0, 6/0 or 3/0.
**Weight:** Lead wire generously applied.
**Tail:** Two dark brown goose biots.
**Abdomen:** Black yarn twisted for a segmented look.
**Wing Case:** Mottled turkey quill section.
**Hackle:** Furnace or brown, palmered over thorax.
**Thorax:** Black dubbing.

## 3. GREEN DAMSEL
*Polly Rosborough*

**Hook:** Regular wire, 3X long, sizes 12 to 8.
**Thread:** Olive 8/0 or 6/0.
**Tail:** Tuft of olive marabou fibers.
**Body:** Light-olive fur (natural or synthetic).
**Beard:** Olive-dyed fibers of guinea, teal, or mallard.
**Wing Case:** Olive marabou tied in at head only.
**Comments:** Imitates the nymph of the damsel fly. I like to shear off the tail and wing case with my thumbnail.

## 4. MATT'S FUR
*Matt Lavell*

**Hook:** Heavy wire, 3X to 6X long, sizes 12 to 6.
**Thread:** Brown 8/0, 6/0, or 3/0.
**Weight:** Lead wire.
**Tail:** Mallard dyed to wood-duck color.
**Rib:** Oval gold tinsel.
**Abdomen and Thorax:** Half-and-half otter and cream seal dubbing.
**Wing Case:** Mallard dyed to wood-duck color.
**Legs:** Tips of wing-case fibers drawn to sides.
**Comments:** Create the wing case and legs as you did for the Pheasant Tail. The Matt's Fur can imitate mayfly or stonefly nymphs.

## 5. OLIVE SCUD

**Hook:** Heavy wire, 1X or 2X long, sizes 16 to 8.
**Thread:** Olive 8/0 or 6/0.
**Weight:** Lead wire (optional).
**Tail:** Olive hackle fibers (or substitute other olive fibers).
**Shellback:** Strip of clear plastic from a plastic bag (a moderately thick plastic).

**Body:** Olive dubbing picked out between ribs.
**Rib:** Fine copper wire.
**Antennae:** (optional) Olive hackle fibers or substitute.
**Comments:** The plastic strip is pulled over the dubbed body and tied down just behind the eye, and then the wire is ribbed up both. Scuds are a common trout food on lakes and slow streams.

## 6. SKIP NYMPH (regular)
*Skip Morris*

**Hook:** Heavy wire, 1X or 2X long, sizes 20 to 8.
**Thread:** Brown 8/0 or 6/0.
**Abdomen and Thorax:** Natural hare's mask.
**Rib:** Copper wire.
**Tail:** Pheasant-tail fibers, split.
**Weight:** The same copper wire used for the rib; for heavy weighting, use lead wire. Any weight is optional.
**Wing Case:** The butts of the pheasant-tail fibers used for the tail, tied in light side up.

## 7. RED FOX SQUIRREL HAIR NYMPH
*Dave Whitlock*

**Hook:** Heavy, regular, or light wire, 2X or 3X long, sizes 18 to 2.
**Thread:** Black 8/0 or 6/0.
**Weight:** Lead wire.
**Tail:** Red-fox-squirrel back hair and underfur.
**Rib:** Fine or very fine oval gold tinsel.
**Abdomen:** Half-and-half mix of red-fox belly hair and a similar color of antron or orlon dubbing.
**Thorax:** Red-fox-squirrel back hair.

## 8. T.D.C.
*Richard Thompson*

**Hook:** Regular or heavy wire, regular shank or 1X long, sizes 20 to 8.
**Thread:** Black 8/0 or 6/0.
**Rib:** Fine flat or oval silver tinsel.
**Abdomen:** Black dubbing, floss. or yarn.
**Thorax:** Black dubbing applied heavily, or chenille.
**Collar:** White ostrich herl.
**Comments:** Imitates the immature form of a chironomid (midge). Designed for lakes. Fish it with very little motion.

## 9. ZUG BUG

**Hook:** Heavy wire, regular shank or 1X long, sizes 16 to 8.
**Thread:** Black 8/0 or 6/0.
**Weight:** Lead wire (optional).
**Tail:** Peacock-herl tips (often, the fibers for this tail come from a peacock feather called a "sword").
**Rib:** Oval silver tinsel
**Body:** Peacock herl.
**Beard:** Brown or furnace hen-hackle fibers; may also be wrapped as a collar in the same manner used for a soft hackle.
**Wing Case:** Tip of a mallard, or mallard dyed wood-duck color, tied in flat and then snipped straight across.

Jim Schollmeyer Photo

# ADDITIONAL BUCKTAILS, STREAMERS, & SOFT HACKLES

## 1. BLACK NOSE DACE
*Art Flick*

**Hook:** Any streamer-bucktail style hook, sizes 4 to 14.
**Thread:** Black 8/0 or 6/0.
**Tail:** Red wool yarn cut short.
**Body:** Flat or embossed silver tinsel.
**Wing:** From bottom to top: white bucktail or calf tail, black bear hair (or substitute, such as black skunk), brown bucktail.
   **Comments:** Fish this as you would any bucktail or steamer.

## 2. BLACK WOOLLY BUGGER

**Hook:** Any streamer-bucktail style hook, sizes 12 to 2.
**Thread:** Black 8/0, 6/0, or 3/0.
**Tail:** Black marabou plume.
**Hackle:** Black, palmered.
**Body:** Black chenille.
   **Comments:** You see—I told you the Woolly Bugger comes in other colors. This is still just the beginning; there are no limits.

## 3. LITTLE RAINBOW TROUT

**Hook:** Any streamer-bucktail style hook, sizes 14 to 4.
**Thread:** Black 8/0 or 6/0.
**Tail:** Green hackle fibers or hair.
**Rib:** Fine flat silver tinsel.
**Body:** Pink dubbing.
**Throat:** Pink bucktail or calf tail.
**Wing:** From bottom to top: white, pink, and green bucktail or calf tail (or all mixed) topped with badger guard hairs.
**Cheeks:** Jungle cock or substitute (I always consider cheeks optional).
   **Comments:** The name tells all; just fish it as though it was a tiny trout.

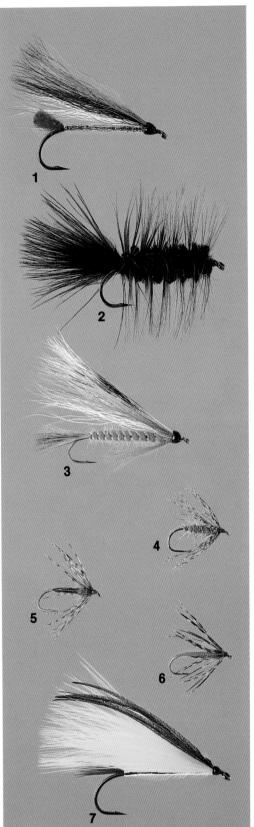

Jim Schollmeyer Photo

## 4. MARCH BROWN SPIDER

**Hook:** Any dry-fly or nymph hook, sizes 18 to 10.
**Thread:** Orange 8/0 or 6/0.
**Body:** Hare's mask dubbing.
**Hackle:** Brown Partridge (or hen saddle, but partridge is shown).
   **Comments:** To quote Dave Hughes from his *American Fly Tying Manual:* "This is the author's very favorite fly for searching a riffle or run when no insects are hatching and no trout are rising." The March Brown Spider also demonstrates that soft hackles needn't always have bodies of floss.

## 5. PARTRIDGE AND GREEN SOFT HACKLE

**Hook:** Any dry-fly or nymph hook, sizes 18 to 10.
**Thread:** Olive or green 8/0 or 6/0.
**Abdomen:** Green floss.
**Thorax:** Hare's mask.
**Hackle:** Gray partridge (or hen saddle).
   **Comments:** Yet another soft hackle, and worth having.

## 6. PARTRIDGE AND ORANGE SOFT HACKLE

**Hook:** Any dry-fly or nymph hook, sizes 18 to 10.
**Thread:** Orange (or pale) 8/0 or 6/0.
**Abdomen:** Orange floss.
**Thorax:** Hare's mask dubbing.
**Hackle:** Brown partridge (or hen saddle).
   **Comments:** The orange in this fly tends to make it a caddis imitation, but there *are* orange stoneflies.

## 7. YELLOW MARABOU

**Hook:** Any streamer-bucktail hook, sizes 12 to 4.
**Thread:** Black 8/0 or 6/0.
**Tail:** Red hackle fibers.
**Body:** Flat or embossed silver tinsel.
**Wing:** Yellow marabou topped with six strands of peacock herl.
   **Comments:** Flashy; sometimes flashy works.

# ADDITIONAL DRY FLIES

## 1. ADAMS PARACHUTE

**Hook:** Dry fly, sizes 16 to 10.
**Thread:** Gray 8/0 or 6/0.
**Wing:** White calf tail.
**Hackle:** Brown and grizzly.
**Tail:** Brown and grizzly hackle fibers or moose body.
**Body:** Muskrat fur dubbing.
   **Comments:** As with the Light Cahill Parachute, almost any dry fly can be converted to a parachute. Wind the two hackles one at a time, and leave a space between turns of the first hackle to accommodate the second.

## 2. BAETIS COMPARADUN

**Hook:** Dry fly, sizes 22 to 16.
**Thread:** Olive 8/0 or 6/0.
**Wing:** Gray deer hair.
**Tail:** Medium blue dun hackle fibers, split.
**Body:** Gray-olive dubbing.
   **Comments:** My own Comparadun solution to the ubiquitous baetis mayfly hatch, also called the blue-wing olive hatch.

## 3. BLONDE WULFF

*Lee Wulff*
**Hook:** Dry fly, sizes 16 to 6.
**Thread:** Tan 8/0 or 8/0.
**Wing:** Light tan deer or elk hair.
**Tail:** Light tan deer or elk hair.
**Body:** Light tan dubbing
**Hackle:** Ginger.

## 4. DARK STONE

*Polly Rosborough*
**Hook:** Long-shank dry-fly hook, sizes 8 and 6.
**Thread:** Black 8/0 or 6/0.
**Rib:** Furnace hackle.
**Body:** Orange synthetic yarn (or substitute orange dubbing).
**Wing:** Brown bucktail.
**Hackle:** Furnace.

## 5. DEER HAIR CADDIS

**Hook:** Dry fly, 20 to 10.
**Thread:** Gray.
**Body:** Olive Dubbing.
**Hackle:** Blue dun.
**Wing:** Natural gray deer hair.
   **Comments:** Tie the hackle in at the bend, then palmer it up the body. Trim the hackle flat underneath, in line with the hook's point. This fly was made popular by my friend Jim Schollmeyer. Though a keen fisherman, Jim's greatest gift is his ability to capture fly fishing on film.

## 6. GINGER QUILL

**Hook:** Dry fly, sizes 20 to 10.
**Thread:** Yellow or tan.
**Wing:** Duck quill.
**Tail:** Ginger hackle fibers.
**Body:** Stripped peacock quill.
**Hackle:** Ginger.

## 7. GREEN DRAKE

**Hook:** Dry fly, sizes 14 to 10.
**Thread:** Olive 8/0 or 6/0.
**Wing:** Natural gray deer hair.

Jim Schollmeyer Photo

**Tail:** Gray deer hair or natural moose body.
**Body:** Olive dubbing.
**Rib:** Yellow floss (optional).
**Hackle:** Grizzly and brown (or grizzly dyed yellow, or one yellow and one grizzly—no one's too sure on this one).
   **Comments:** Optional rib, all sorts of hackle choices, even some discrepancy regarding name as this fly is sometimes called the Western Green Drake and is sometimes confused or simply blended with a fly called the Green Drake Wulff—many flies fall into such confusion. This happens most often when a fly evolves gradually through various tiers; local variations abound, and no one can say just what's right.

## 8. HENRYVILLE SPECIAL

*Hiram Brobst*
**Hook:** Dry fly, sizes 20 to 14.
**Rib:** Grizzly hackle, one size smaller than hook, palmered.
**Body:** Green floss or dubbing.
**Under Wing:** Wood-duck fibers.
**Wing:** Duck-quill sections cupped over the body.
**Hackle:** Brown.
   **Comments:** It can help to trim the palmered hackle a bit on top before tying in the wings. The wood-duck under wing is tied as a small bunch; the wings are tied in using the pinch, butts forward.

## 9. LIGHT CAHILL

*Dan Cahill*
**Hook:** Dry fly, sizes 20 to 10.
**Thread:** Cream 8/0 or 6/0.
**Wing:** Wood-duck.
**Tail:** Ginger hackle fibers.
**Body:** Cream badger underfur dubbed.
**Hackle:** Ginger.

## 10. POLY WING SPINNER

**Hook:** Dry fly, sizes 24 to 10.
**Thread:** Color to match body, 8/0 or 6/0.
**Tail:** Hackle fibers of body color, split.
**Abdomen and Thorax:** Dubbing of appropriate color.
**Wing:** Poly yarn tied flat across thorax (usually gray).
   **Comments:** I find it easiest to tie in the tails and dub the thorax before tying in and dubbing around the wings. The wings are tied in on top of the thorax with figure-eight thread wraps; the wings are a single length of poly yarn.
   The poly yarn spinner imitates a spent, dying mayfly that has dropped her eggs. The spinner flights of mayflies are often of great interest to trout and, therefore, anglers. The Poly Wing Spinner is tied in a variety of shades and sizes to imitate mayfly spinners.

## 11. RED QUILL

*Art Flick*
**Hook:** Dry fly, sizes 18 to 12.
**Thread:** Gray 8/0 or 6/0.
**Wing:** Wood-duck.
**Tail:** Blue-dun hackle fibers.
**Body:** Stem (or stems) from a brown hackle.
**Hackle:** Medium blue dun.

# BASIC PRINCIPLES OF FLY TYING

Most of what I am about to discuss will apply to every fly you tie. There is experience here and, I hope, a bit of wisdom.

### Taper Most Cuts

Usually, the things you cut and trim on a fly will be wrapped over with something—thread, yarn, dubbing, ribbing—and it is always easier to wrap over a taper than a shelf. Wing butts, tail butts, hackle stems, almost everything should be trimmed to a taper. This is especially true if a section of the fly is to be formed over the cut end of something; the body of the Light Cahill Parachute, for example, is formed over the cut ends of the calf-tail wing—blunt-cut wing butts will create a lumpy body, but cut these wing butts at an angle and your Light Cahill Parachute will have a smoothly tapered body.

### Avoid Gaps

If you cut the wing butts of your Gray Wulff short and steep and you do the same with the tail butts, you will have a gap between the two consisting of only shank and a bit of thread. The body you dub over this foundation will also have a gap; this body will also be awkward to form and have a lumpy appearance. If you try to fill in the gap with extra dubbing, there will be a lump beneath the filled gap—that's because the gap is only on top of the shank. If, however, you blend the tapered ends of the wings and tail, this smooth foundation will produce a smoothly tapered body. Always avoid gaps if at all possible.

### Fix Mistakes When They Happen

Fix mistakes instead of trying to compensate for them later. If you discover that the ends of the second layer of lead on a Morristone are too close to the ends of the first layer, it is faster and easier to unwrap the thread securing that lead and then remove a turn or two than it is to struggle with trying to make the yarn wrap up the steep incline created by the too-close lead ends. You will inevitably discover exceptions with experience, but this rule almost always holds true.

### Tie Tight Flies

This rule harks back to my original list of essential guidelines. To test your flies for tightness, hold the hook firmly by its bend and then try to twist the materials around the shank; they will probably twist, but do they twist easily or reluctantly?

### Tie Several Flies Of One Pattern And Size Per Session

This will vary with experience—for the beginner, two or three flies will easily take up a half hour, but in the same amount of time a professional tier might produce a dozen flies or more. The point is that repetition teaches, and that it will minimize the time required to gather and prepare materials. It also helps to lay out and prepare the materials for the flies you will tie before you have tied even one—efficiency.

### Have Out Only The Tools And Materials You Need

Searching for your hackle pliers or muskrat patch in a pile of materials may make you decide to forget tying an Adams altogether; keep your tools and materials sorted, and place at hand only those you need for the pattern you're tying.

### Determine The Sizes Of Your Thread Heads

This is a personal matter, but there are considerations. Generally, the best tiers create small heads on their flies, though some fine tiers prefer large heads. First there is function—will a tiny head really hold secure a hard and somewhat slick bucktail wing; and if it won't, is a very large head necessary? These things are worked out with time and experience. The heads pictured in this book are my own preference for each fly.

Second, there is aesthetics—should the head be as small as possible so long as it will hold everything together, or should head size, beyond function, be a matter of what suits you? I lean towards the latter. At one time I tied the heads on my display dry flies so small that they all but disappeared; now they are small, but apparent.

### Dark Fly, Light Background Light Fly, Dark Background

Contrast will really help you see your work. Keep sheets of dark and light paper on hand to lay behind your vise; sometimes even a hackle neck or fur patch of appropriate hue behind your fly will provide the needed contrast.

### Develop Your Sense Of Proportion And Style

Stop now and then to inspect a fly—do you like the length of the wings, the thickness of them, the taper of the body? What do you think of other tier's flies?

### Good Flies Catch Fish

Your flies can be a bit rough and still catch fish as well as better tied flies; fish are really less discerning than anglers about fly aesthetics. If your flies are durable and have reasonable proportions, then they are good flies.

### Enjoy Fly Tying

This is a hobby, an art—rather than struggle with it, take your time, enjoy fly tying. As your skills develop you will probably enjoy tying more and more—that's how it's gone for me. You will fall into a rhythm as you tie and discover how to adjust your flies to your tastes and needs—just how thick should the hackles on your Elk Hair Caddises be for your favorite stream, and how much lead is best for the Gold Ribbed Hare's Ears you will fish there? At some point you will discover, as all tiers do, that fly patterns aren't holy—you can alter them, change colors, materials, proportions. You can be creative in fly tying and that is part of the enjoyment.

# ESSENTIAL ENTOMOLOGY

Illustrations by Skip Morris

We, fly fishers tend to divide flies that imitate insects into two categories: nymphs and dry flies. Real insects often have more stages than this. When an insect shifts from its underwater stage to its winged adult stage, it is "hatching." When many identical insects are hatching at once, we call this a "hatch." Here is a scan of the common trout-food insects whose hatching creates hatches:

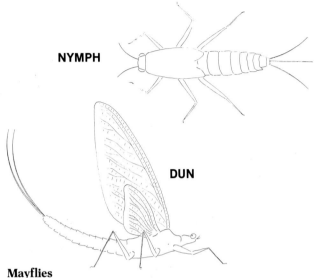

### Mayflies

The "nymph," the immature underwater version of many aquatic insects, composes the bulk of a fly's life; the mayfly "dun," the freshly hatched adult, can be recognized by its upright wings that, when together, look like a tiny sail; the mayfly "spinner," the mating or mated adult that soon dies, will look much like the dun though there may be differences in color. Mayflies run from tiny to large, pale to dark in a variety of colors, and live in all kinds of water from still to fast.

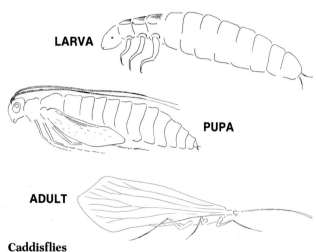

### Caddisflies

A caddisfly lives most of its life under water as a "larva," an immature form; it matures partially and then ascends to the water's surface as a "pupa"; as a winged adult, it returns to the surface to drink or release eggs. Caddisfly adults hold their wings tentlike back over their bodies, and come in as wide a range of sizes, colors, and habitats as do mayflies.

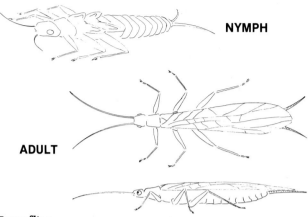

### Stoneflies

A stonefly lives most of its life as a nymph, and then crawls to stream side to shed its shuck and take wing. The adult stonefly holds its wings flat, back over its body. Although stoneflies vary in size and color as do mayflies and caddisflies, stoneflies live only in moving water, usually swift.

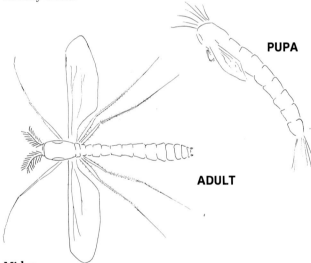

### Midge

Though they are usually tiny, mosquitolike midges are important to the trout fisher. They follow the same larva-pupa-adult cycle as does the caddis. Midges like water that is still or slow.

### Fish

Minnows, sculpins, and tiny trout are among the fishes that trout eat and fly fishers imitate with streamers and bucktails.

### Others

There are other trout-food insects of importance that is occasional, regional, or both. These include the slow-to-still-water dwelling damselfly, dragonfly, and backswimmer. "Terrestrial," land-living, insects such as grasshoppers, ants, beetles, and the like can sometimes hold trout's attention. And there are yet other insects and creatures even less often worth notice by the fly fisher. But day in and day out, mayflies, caddisflies, and stoneflies are the trout's fare and the fly fisher's models.